PLAYS FOR LEARNING
Ancient Israel

Legends from the Bible and Jewish Folklore for Grades K–3

by L.E. McCullough, Ph.D.

YOUNG ACTORS SERIES

A Smith and Kraus Book

A Smith and Kraus Book
Published by Smith and Kraus, Inc.
177 Lyme Road, Hanover, NH 03755

Copyright ©2001 by L.E. McCullough
All rights reserved
Manufactured in the United States of America

First Edition: March 2001
10 9 8 7 6 5 4 3 2 1

LIMITED REPRODUCTION PERMISSION:
The publisher grants permission to individual teachers to reproduce the scripts as needed for use with their own students. Permission for reproduction for an entire school district or for commercial use is required. Also, permission for public readings must be secured. Please call Smith and Kraus, Inc at (603) 643-6431.

Cover and Text Design by
Julia Hill Gignoux, Freedom Hill Design

The Library of Congress Cataloging-In-Publication Data
McCullough, L.E.
Plays of ancient Israel : legends from the Bible and Jewish folklore / by L.E. McCullough.
p. cm.
Includes bibliographical references (p.).
ISBN 1-57525-252-X
1. Bible. O.T.—History of Biblical events—Juvenile drama. 2. Judaism—History—To 70 A.D.—Juvenile drama. 3. Jews—History—To 70 A.D.—Juvenile drama. 4. Children's plays, American. 5. Religious drama, American. 6. Bible plays, American. [1. Bible. O.T.—Drama. 2. Jews—History—To 70 A.D.—Drama. 3. Bible plays. 4. Plays.] I. Title.

PS3563.C35297 P58535 2000
812'.54—dc21   00-067972

This book is dedicated to all those throughout history who have searched with diligence and compassion for truth, for justice, for a way to comprehend and share the unfathomable mystery of the universe and use that knowledge to transform this Earth into the Divine Paradise the Creator has always intended.

And to my wife, Lisa Bansavage, who has filled my world with beauty, bounty, and blessings.

Acknowledgments

Dr. Miles Krassen;
Chana Mlotek, Music Archivist, YIVO Institute for Jewish Research;
Rev. T.H. Gillespie, Memorial Baptist Church;
Monsignor James Higgins;
Dr. Harry and Jackie Wolf, Beth-El Zedeck Temple;
Dr. Gerald Epstein, D.D.S;
Rabbi Israel P. Feinhandler, Jerusalem;
Nancy and George Balderose.

CONTENTS

Foreword vi
A Note on Costumes, Sets, and Music xi
Introduction xiii

King David's Harp 1
Jonah and the Whale 14
Noah's Ark: Falsehood and Wickedness
   Hitch a Ride 30
Dare to Be a Daniel! 38
Ruth and Naomi: The Healing Power
   of Friendship 54
Samson and Delilah 63
Tales of Angels 78
What Is a Brother? 88
The Prophet and The Rabbi 101
The Wisdom of Solomon 110
Chanukah: Come Light the Menorah! 125
Hail, Queen Esther! 142

FOREWORD

Israel shall be a proverb and a byword among all people.
                                                    I Kings, 9:7

What is hateful to you do not do to your neighbor. That is the whole Torah. The rest is commentary.
                        Hillel, Jewish scholar, 1st century B.C.E.

Other books were given to us for information. The Bible was given for transformation.
                                                        Anonymous

The land of Israel is the birthplace of two major religions (Judaism and Christianity) that inspired a third (Islam). The twelve plays in this book celebrate one of the greatest sources of faith and legend in the world — the Tanakh, or Old Testament, of the Bible. As many modern writers have shown, myths and tales are not simply escapist fantasy; they are one of the chief ways a child learns about the adult world and how to live in it.

Bible stories not only transmit points of belief or doctrine but communicate essential relationships about human nature. As a child, the Bible was the first book of truly grown-up stories I remember reading. Mother Goose and Dr. Seuss were entertaining in their clever way, but Bible stories had sticking power. Talk about *Adventure* with a Capital A! Adam and Eve, Cain and Abel, David and Goliath, Samson and Delilah, Sodom and Gomorrah and all that sea-parting, lion-smiting, jawbone-bashing, bush-burning derring-do — the eternal cosmic struggle between good and evil played out in the mundane lives of ordinary men and women, earthbound but always seeking the promise of salvation beckoning beyond the stars.

Added to the Biblical base are legends from the Midrash, a body of Jewish sacred and legal literature intended to offer in-depth interpretations of the Scriptures and Judaic religious law. *Midrashim* are to the basic Bible tale as a blueberry cheese knish is to a plain potato — layer upon layer of extra richness and flavor embroidering the core text.

Plays of Ancient Israel will not only be of interest to followers of Judaism and Christianity. The stories dramatized here are part of world mythology and world history, among the earliest efforts to celebrate and explain humanity's ongoing relationship with the divine. It is my hope that *Plays of Ancient Israel* will make these stories more accessible to readers of all religious affiliations, to spread the wonder inherent in these larger-than-life tales of faith and — in some cases — incontrovertible fact.

Plays of Ancient Israel can also be combined with studies in other disciplines: history, science, language arts, dance, music, social studies, and so forth. The plays are set in the ancient Middle East; feel free to decorate the set with architecture, plants, and art objects specific to that region. If you are a music teacher and want to add songs and music to any of the plays, go ahead and make it a class project by organizing a chorus or having students select appropriate recordings to play before and after the performance.

Besides those children enrolled in the onstage cast, others can be included in the production as lighting and sound technicians, prop masters, script coaches and stage managers. *Plays of Ancient Israel* is an excellent vehicle for getting other members of the school and community involved in your project. Maybe there are Jewish or Middle Eastern dance troupes or accomplished performers of Jewish or

Middle Eastern music in your area; ask them to give a special concert or lecture when you present the play. There are undoubtedly several knowledgeable scholars at your local library, art museum, synagogue, church, or college who can add interesting tidbits about the customs and folklore that provide background for these tales. Try utilizing the talents of local school or youth orchestra members to play incidental music. . . get the school art club to paint scrims and backdrops. . . see if a senior citizens' group might volunteer time to sew costumes. . . inquire whether any local restaurants might bring samples of Jewish or Middle Eastern cuisine.

Most of all, have lots of fun. Realizing that many performing groups may have limited technical and space resources, I have kept sets, costumes, and props minimal. However, if you do have the ability to build a seaworthy sailing vessel for *Noah's Ark: Falsehood and Wickedness Hitch a Ride* or can fashion a facsimile of a Persian palace for *Hail, Queen Esther!* — go for it! Adding more music, dance, and visual arts and crafts into the production involves more children and makes your play a genuinely multimedia event.

Similarly, I have supplied only basic stage and lighting directions. Blocking is really the province of the director; once you get the play up and moving, feel free to suit cast and action to your available population and experience level of actors. When figuring out how to stage these plays, I suggest you follow the venerable UYI Method — Use Your Imagination. If the play calls for a boat, bring in a wood frame, an old bathtub, or have children draw a boat and hang it as a scrim behind where the actors perform. Keep in mind the spirit of the old Andy Hardy musicals: "C'mon, everybody! Let's make a show!"

Age and gender. Obviously, your purpose in putting on the play is to entertain as well as educate. Even though one typically thinks of palace guards and prophets as being male, there is no reason these roles can't be played in *your* production by females; likewise this can be true for other gender-free representations of angels, spirits, and Voices of God. After all, the essence of the theatrical experience is to suspend us in time and ask us to believe that anything may be possible. Once again, UYI! Adult characters, such as grandparents and "old wise men/women" can certainly be played by children costumed or made up to fit the part as closely as possible, or they can actually be played by adults. While *Plays of Ancient Israel* are intended to be performed chiefly by young people, moderate adult involvement will add validation and let children know this isn't just a "kid project." If you want to get very highly choreographed or musically intensive, you will probably find a strategically placed onstage adult or two very helpful in keeping things moving smoothly. Still, *never* underestimate the capacity for even the youngest children to amaze you with their skill and ingenuity in making a show blossom.

Plays of Ancient Israel is a fun way to introduce children to one of the richest traditions in world literature. And for adults, these plays offer a chance to recapture the joy and excitement we all felt the first time we heard the thrilling words "In the beginning God created the heavens and earth. . ." Who says you can't be a kid again? Just heed the call of the shofar and follow the animals two by two. . . mind that burning bush lurking 'round the corner!

L.E. McCullough, Ph.D.
Humanities Theatre Group
Indiana University-Purdue University at Indianapolis
Indianapolis, Indiana

A NOTE ON COSTUMES, SETS, AND MUSIC

These plays are set in an "Old Testament time" period that most closely corresponds in real cultural and costume details to approximately 500–2500 B.C.E. Here are some sources for finding costume ideas that are fairly authentic to the ancient Middle East (library call number in bold):

- *A History of Jewish Costume* by Alfred Rubens. New York, Funk & Wagnalls, 1967. **GT540.R73**

- *Costuming the Biblical Play* by Lucy Barton. Boston: Walter H. Baker Co., 1962. **792.026**. This is *the* most detailed work in the field by a renowned costume historian but it may be hard to find. It has suggested costumings for a huge array of Old Testament characters from Ruth and Moses to angels and Roman soldiers.

- *Costume of Old Testament Peoples* by Philip J. Watson. Edgemont, Penn.: Chelsea House, 1987. **391.093**. An excellent survey of ancient Middle Eastern costume, hairstyles, and materials with a chapter on the Israelites and their neighbors.

- *Historic Costume for the Stage* by Lucy Barton. Boston: Walter H. Baker Co., 1961. **792.0261961BAR**. The most comprehensive book on historic costume. This includes material on Old Testament costume not covered in Barton's book above, in addition to other ancient and medieval attire.

- *20,000 Years of Fashion* by François Boucher. New York: Harry N. Abrams, 1987. **391.09**. This has a special chapter on Jewish Costume.

- *A Survey of Historical Costume* by Phyllis Tertora and Keith Eubank. New York: Fairchild Publishers, 1990. 391.009.

- *What People Wore: A Visual History of Dress from Ancient Times to 20th-Century America* by Douglas Gorsline. New York: Dover Press, 1999. 391.09. This has a *huge* bibliography of other costume books.

- *Costumes and Settings for Staging Historical Plays, Vol. I The Classical Period* by Jack Cassin-Scott. Boston: Plays, Inc. 391. Cas. Excellent material on ancient Middle Eastern stage properties, accessories, design, costume, architecture.

To decorate your scrims and background sets, Dover also publishes iron-on transfer books of gargoyles and folklore creatures, angels, wild animals — plus calligraphy, floral patterns, and ornamental designs from cultures around the world including Middle Eastern and Old European.

Using authentic ethnic or period music is a great way to enhance your production. The public library is always a good source, yet recordings of folk and ethnic international music are increasingly more available at mainstream record stores and from catalogues. If you have questions about where to find recordings or written music of the tunes or genres included in these plays, or want some tips on performing and arranging them, I would be happy to assist you and may be reached by calling Smith and Kraus, Inc. at their toll-free customer service number, 1-800-895-4331.

INTRODUCTION

Religious education, regardless of denominational affiliation, is an extraordinary challenge. The demands placed on our children are quite heavy when they enter our churches and synagogues on Sunday morning. These include a competitive academic world, extra-curricular activities such as sports, music lessons, and of course, numerous social obligations (Saturday night sleepovers are the curse of the Sunday school teacher). Moreover, we live in a world of multi-media and twenty-second attention spans. When religious school begins, our students have a skeptical look that says, "What am I doing here?"

Those of us committed to religious education address this question each week in our lesson plans. Hence, we are always on the lookout for new resources that will engage our students on two levels. One is to make it fun by making the timeless stories of our Scriptures "come alive" through imagination and involvement. The second (and most important) is to engage our students on a spiritual, moral, and ethical level. Such resources are scarce.

This work, *Plays for Learning Ancient Israel: Legends from the Bible and Jewish Folklore,* will greatly assist those engaged in this sacred task. Taking popular, well-known stories, such as Noah's Ark and Jonah and the Whale, as well as some lesser-known ones, such as Ruth and Naomi, the author recasts these treasures in a play format that can be performed by young and old alike. He does so in a fun and creative way, yet even for the novice teacher these plays are quite easy to plan. Each play contains directions, including stage sets, cast, effects, props, and even a list of costumes. Simply put, the plays are fun to read and one can easily see students and adults "hamming it up."

The beauty of this work is the seamless way in which it encourages the performers to think of the deeper meaning of the Biblical narrative. In one of my favorite plays, *Noah's Ark: Falsehood and Wickedness Hitch a Ride,* we're introduced to the idea of Midrash; that there contains a hidden meaning in this story of destruction and survival. At the center of the play, "Falsehood" and "Wickedness" hitch a ride on the ark to survive the flood. In order to gain entry, they must enter into a contract (all the animals travel in pairs, so they must form a partnership). The deal is that if they survive the flood, all profit or gain achieved by Falsehood will be turned over to Wickedness.

We see from this play that Professor L.E. McCullough is teaching the story on two levels. One is the narrative. There is the flood and Noah must gather all the animals to save the world from destruction. By introducing "Falsehood" and "Wickedness" into the account, the student begins to appreciate the Flood story on a deeper level. There is neither profit nor gain where one commits a falsehood in order to advance his or her own position in life. By performing, observing, and discussing Scripture in this form, students and teachers alike focus on the ethical and moral lessons essential for a life of meaning.

This book is a resource that addresses the problem of boredom and disinterest in Sunday school. It moves the educator away from being perceived as "preaching" to one that is involved with students in doing something that is fun and engaging, and most important, in exploring the connection between our spirituality and our ethical and moral responsibilities to our world.

Rabbi Edward Boraz, Ph.D.
February 7, 2001

KING DAVID'S HARP

Living in the 10th century B.C.E. King David was a brave warrior, a skilled general, and powerful king, but he was also a poet and musician and composer of more than half of the 150 Psalms, among the oldest prayers mentioned in the Bible. The Psalms are short, pithy conversations with God that express a wide range of emotions and present many aspects of humanity's relationship with God. Some of the Psalms were annotated with the Hebrew word *mizmor*, meaning that they were to be sung and accompanied by an instrument, most likely a harp — an instrument King David was said to have played. What would King David's harp have looked like? The Hebrew word for harp, *kinnor*, is mentioned frequently in the Old Testament yet, unfortunately, never described. Scholars believe it was similar to the *kithara*, a Greek harp popular throughout the ancient Middle East. The *kithara* was a box lyre made of wood, strung with 3–12 sheep-gut strings. It was played either with the fingers or with a plectrum. For more information about ancient Jewish and Middle Eastern music, consult these three books: *The Music of the Bible Revealed* by Suzanne Haik-Vantoura; *David's Harp: The Story of Music in Biblical Times* by Alfred Sendrey and Mildred Norton; *Heritage of Music: The Music of the Jewish People* by Judith Kaplan Eisenstein.

STAGE SET: A living room chair at down right; wooden bench at down left; scrim at mid center with slides or drawings of harps (*kinnor*) hanging from tree branches

CAST: 7 actors, minimum 2 boys (•), 4 girls (+) plus Offstage Chorus

- + Mother
- + Miriam
- + Hodevah's Daughter Guide
- • Hodevah
- + Hodevah's Wife
- • Hodevah's Son

MUSIC: "Harp Excerpts #1–4;" Psalm 92

PROPS: Violin; book; walking stick; *kinnor**

COSTUMES: Mother and Miriam wear modern clothes. Hodevah, Hodevah's Wife, Hodevah's Son, and Hodevah's Daughter wear basic Biblical attire — long-sleeved, plain-colored tunics (ankle-length for females, knee-length for males), sandals, a simple cloth or scarf wrapped around the head and shoulders for Hodevah's Wife, beards for adult men. Guide wears a long hooded robe or cloak, sandals.

Note: While Miriam is supposed to be a novice violinist, it would be great if the actor playing her were actually a moderately skilled violinist who can pretend to perform poorly at the start of the play, then lead off Psalm 92 at the end and perform competently along with the song. If a violinist isn't available, miming and syncing to a tape is fine.

* A simple *kinnor* is easy and fun to make. Several forms of this instrument existed in ancient times, but it's basically a hollow wooden box (12" wide x 12" high x 2" deep) with two vertical side bars (15") united by a horizontal cross bar. You can make the frame out of metal or wooden dowel rods not more than 2" in diameter, and the strings can be gut, wire or nylon. Add tuning pegs where the strings connect to the crossbar and paint a design on the sound box if you wish.

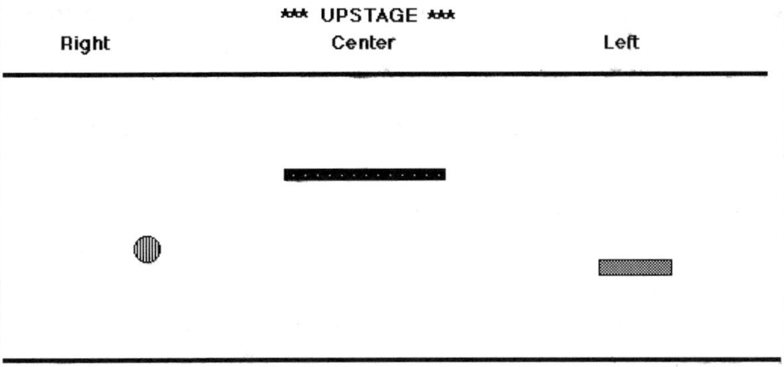

```
*** UPSTAGE ***
Right          Center                    Left
```

Stage Plan— *King David's Harp*

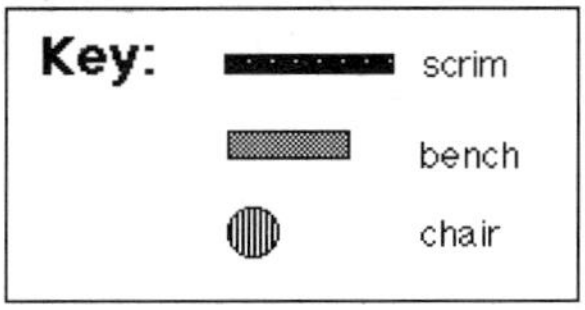

Key:
▬▬▬ scrim
▬ bench
◉ chair

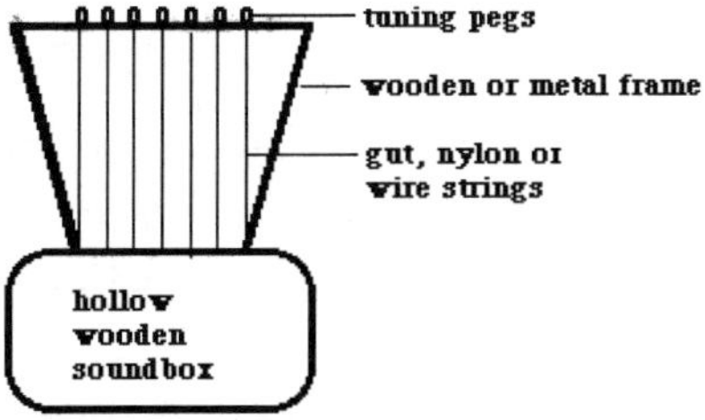

KINNOR
after model in Palestinian
Archeological Museum, Jerusalem

(tuning pegs / wooden or metal frame / gut, nylon or wire strings / hollow wooden soundbox)

(LIGHTS UP DOWN RIGHT ON MIRIAM standing at down right, painfully practicing violin; MOTHER sits a few feet up left, reading a book. Miriam's playing is very rudimentary, and she finally stops in frustration and wails.)

King David's Harp 3

MIRIAM: Aauugghh! This is torture! How can any human stand the sound of me practicing the violin? *I* can't even stand it!

MOTHER: It sounds lovely, Miriam. And the more you practice, the better you'll become.

MIRIAM: The more I practice, the quicker I'll become insane! Mother, why do I have to play a musical instrument?

MOTHER: Music is a wonderful way to speak to God. It was Rabbi Uri of Strelisk who once said, "Of all the halls of Heaven, the hall of music is the smallest, but anyone who wants to approach God has only to enter this hall."

MIRIAM: Where do people get these weird ideas about music being heavenly? *(brandishes violin)* Not from this thing!

MOTHER: The idea of music serving as a pathway to heaven has been around a long time. *(holds up book)* Right here in Psalm 81 it says, "Sing aloud to God for our strength; shout for joy to the God of Jacob." In fact, once there was a man named Hodevah who found God through music.

(LIGHTS FADE OUT DOWN RIGHT, FADE UP LEFT ON HODEVAH sitting on wooden bench; he holds a kinnor in his lap and is adjusting the strings.)

MOTHER: Hodevah was a maker of musical instruments who lived in Jerusalem some years after the Jews returned the second time from exile in Babylon — more than five hundred years after King David had ruled Israel. Hodevah was a pious man, and his name, in fact, meant "Jehovah is his praise." Whenever he made a new harp, Hodevah could not help but wonder what had become of King David's harp.

HODEVAH: *(regarding the kinnor)* Sing brightly, my wooden friend! If only your melodies could tell where to find your glorious ancestor — the harp of King David — lost these many years! *(plays a quick glissando)* Hmmm.

If King David's harp *could* be found and returned to Jerusalem, the Spirit of God might also return to Israel. *(rises and shouts)* That's it! I will find the harp! I will find King David's harp!

(HODEVAH'S WIFE, HODEVAH'S SON, AND HODEVAH'S DAUGHTER enter from left as Hodevah paces excitedly.)

HODEVAH'S SON: Father, father! What is wrong! Are you ill?

HODEVAH: No, my son, I have never felt better! Quickly, we must prepare!

HODEVAH'S DAUGHTER: Prepare for what, father?

HODEVAH: I must travel to Babylon.

HODEVAH'S WIFE: Babylon! Surely you jest? It is only recently that our people were slaves in Babylon. Why would you want to go there?

HODEVAH: To find King David's harp! And restore the Spirit of God to Israel!

HODEVAH'S WIFE: *(takes him by shoulders and sits him down on bench)* My dearest husband, we all want the Spirit of God to return to Israel. But searching for a harp? In Babylon?

HODEVAH: Do you not remember Psalm 137? "By the rivers of Babylon, there we sat down and there we wept when we remembered Zion. On the willows there we hung up our harps, for there our captors asked us for songs, and our tormentors asked for mirth, saying, 'Sing us one of the songs of Zion!'" The harp of King David must still be in one of the willow trees of Babylon!

HODEVAH'S SON: Father, there are many rivers in Babylon. Which one will you seek?

HODEVAH: Whichever has willow trees on its banks.

HODEVAH'S DAUGHTER: But the rivers of Babylon flow for hundreds of miles and have thousands of willow trees!

HODEVAH: You may doubt the truth of the Psalms, but I believe. Wife, gather my things! There is no more time to waste! *(rises, exits left)*

HODEVAH'S SON: Mother, what can we do to stop him?

HODEVAH'S WIFE: When a servant hears the call of his master, he must follow the summons.

HODEVAH'S DAUGHTER: Then we must pray for his safe journey.

(Hodevah's Wife, Hodevah's Son, and Hodevah's Daughter join hands, bow heads, and pray.)

HODEVAH'S WIFE: Come, bless the Lord, all you servants of the Lord, who stand by night in the house of the Lord! Lift up your hands to the holy place and bless the Lord.

HODEVAH'S SON & HODEVAH'S DAUGHTER: May the Lord, maker of heaven and earth, bless you from Zion.

(LIGHTS OUT; Hodevah's Wife, Hodevah's Son, and Hodevah's Daughter exit left.)

MOTHER: The next day Hodevah left Jerusalem and began walking eastward.

(LIGHTS UP CENTER ON Hodevah trudging wearily in from left, leaning on a walking stick and crossing to down center, peering around him and upward.)

MOTHER: He climbed steep mountains, crossed a scorching desert, made his way slowly through deep wilderness until he reached the sparkling rivers of Babylon. Every step of the way it seemed as if he could almost hear the harp of King David calling, as he searched the branches of willow trees in vain.

HODEVAH: *(stands at down center)* Almighty God, hear the prayers of a weary old man. I fear that I am no closer to finding the harp than the day I left Jerusalem. *(kneels)* Send me a sign before I die in this foreign land.

(MUSIC: Harp music sounds offstage [Harp Excerpt #1]; SPOTLIGHT ON GUIDE, a hooded robed figure standing at down left.)

GUIDE: Hodevah of Jerusalem, you have come upon this journey for the right reasons. But you have searched in the wrong place.

HODEVAH: Who-who are you? Are you a spirit or a man?

GUIDE: I am your guide. Hear my words: The psalm says the harps were hung in the willows of Zion, not Babylon. Do you not remember the words of the Psalm? "How could we sing the Lord's song in a foreign land?" When they were forced into exile, the people left their harps behind. Go, return to your family, and seek the magic harp among the willows of Zion.

(SPOTLIGHT OUT on Guide, who exits left; Hodevah stands and declares to audience.)

HODEVAH: Hear this, all you peoples. Give ear, all inhabitants of the world, both low and high, rich and poor together. My mouth shall speak wisdom, the meditation of my heart shall be understanding. I will incline my ear to a proverb, I will solve my riddle to the music of the harp.

(MUSIC: Harp music sounds offstage [Harp Excerpt #2], LIGHTS OUT as Hodevah exits left.)

MOTHER: Hodevah made his way back to Jerusalem, and this time he was filled with great joy. For he believed that the guide who had spoken to him was none other than the spirit of King David himself!

(LIGHTS UP LEFT ON Hodevah entering down left and rejoining his family.)

HODEVAH'S DAUGHTER: Father! You are alive!

HODEVAH'S SON: Did you find the harp? Did you find it?

HODEVAH: Alas, I did not. My zeal prevented me from thinking clearly. I now believe the harp is here in Zion.

HODEVAH'S WIFE: But where in Zion? We also have thousands of willow trees. Oh, husband, will you not give up this foolish quest and look to your family?

HODEVAH: *(sighs)* My days are like an evening shadow; I wither away like grass. You, O Lord, are enthroned forever. Your name endures to all generations.
(Hodevah's Wife leads Hodevah to the bench and sits him down, his head bowed; Hodevah's Wife, Hodevah's Son, and Hodevah's Daughter exit left.)

MOTHER: Hodevah went back to making his instruments, until after a time he became nearly blind and could work no more. He had given up his dream of finding King David's harp and was simply waiting for life to end. Until one day —

(MUSIC: Harp music sounds offstage [Harp Excerpt #1]; Hodevah rises unsteadily.)

HODEVAH: That music! The music I heard in Babylon! Is it real, or am I only imagining it?

(SPOTLIGHT ON GUIDE standing at down left.)

GUIDE: Follow the music, Hodevah. Arise, and let it lead you to the mountain called Zion.

HODEVAH: But I am old and almost blind! How can I climb up a mountain?

GUIDE: Trust in the Lord, Hodevah! He turns a desert into pools of water, clothes the meadow with flocks, and decks the valley with grain. Can he not lead you up a mountain? *(exits left)*

(LIGHTS UP CENTER as Hodevah walks unsteadily to down center.)

MOTHER: Hodevah journeyed to Mount Zion and — as the guide had said — by the power of God he was able to climb to its peak, as if he were once again a young man. Yet, his joy was short-lived. Though he searched every willow tree, he could find no harp.
HODEVAH: *(kneels at down center)* Lord, remember your word to your servant, in which you have made me hope. This is my comfort in my distress. Your promise gives me life.

(MUSIC: Harp music sounds offstage [Harp Excerpt #3]; Hodevah looks behind him toward mid center.)

MOTHER: This time the music Hodevah heard was very clear and very close by.

(Hodevah approaches the scrim, fumbling as if turning aside the branches of a tree.)

MOTHER: He rose and took a few steps behind in the direction of the music. He discovered the entrance to a cave, covered by a willow tree. Fearlessly, he went inside the cave. And there he came upon the most marvelous sight in all the world.

(SPOTLIGHT ON scrim at mid center showing trees and harps.)

King David's Harp

HODEVAH: A forest of willow trees, each with a harp hanging from its branches making the most beautiful sounds!

(MUSIC: Harp music sounds offstage [Harp Excerpt #4]. SPOTLIGHT NARROWS TO HARP IN CENTER OF SCRIM.)

HODEVAH: And there on the tallest tree is a harp of pure gold! This must be the harp of King David!
MOTHER: Hodevah had indeed found King David's harp. He was so happy, he simply sat down underneath the harp and listened in rapture to the music that had inspired the King to write some of his greatest Psalms.

(Hodevah sits in front of scrim and listens, smiling and with eyes closed, to the harp music LIGHTS FADE OUT CENTER, FADE UP DOWN RIGHT ON Mother and Miriam.)

MOTHER: In fact, some say Hodevah never left the cave on Mount Zion but continued to listen for the rest of his days, sustained by the heavenly music.
MIRIAM: After Hodevah found the harp, did the Spirit of God return to Israel?
MOTHER: Maybe the Spirit of God had never really left, but people forgot where to look. And with music—
MIRIAM: I know, I know. Music is a pathway to heaven. But right now it seems like a major roadblock!
MOTHER: Just keep practicing, dear. And remember Psalm 92:

(Miriam plays introduction to "Psalm 92" and Mother begins singing, joined by Offstage Chorus.)

MOTHER & OFFSTAGE CHORUS: *(sing)*

> It is good to give thanks to the Lord,
> To sing praises to your name, O Most High,
> To declare your steadfast love in the morning
> And your faithfulness by night
> To the music of the lute and the harp,
> To the melody of the lyre.
> For you, O Lord, have made me glad by your work;
> At the works of your hands I sing for joy.

(LIGHTS OUT.)

THE END

Harp Excerpts

Psalm 92

(melody by L.E. McCullough based on ancient Middle Eastern modes)

© L.E. McCullough 2000

King David's Harp 13

JONAH AND THE WHALE

Living during the 8th century B.C.E., when Israel was part of the mighty Assyrian empire, the prophet Jonah hailed from a small village near Nazareth. Jonah's adventures provide a good example of how God often chooses unlikely people to perform important tasks. In addition, the point is made that the message of salvation is not always designed to suit our needs but is often directed toward the needs of others, even our enemies. The story of Jonah is read in synagogues on Yom Kippur, the Day of Atonement, the day in the Jewish calendar when God forgives those who sincerely return to Him.

STAGE SET: A small wooden bench at down left

CAST: 13 actors, minimum 2 boys (•), 1 girl (+)

- Jonah
- Ship Captain
+ Whale
  3 Sailors
  6 Ninevites
  Voice of God (Offstage)

EFFECTS: Visual — lightning flash; Sound — Voice of God should use an offstage microphone with a fair amount of reverb; thunder crack; stormy wind; loud rumble

MUSIC: "Row the Galley;" "Jonah and the Whale"

PROPS: Parchment scroll; a coin

COSTUMES: Characters wear basic Biblical attire — long-sleeved, plain-colored tunics (ankle-length for females, knee-length for males), sandals, a simple cloth or scarf wrapped around the head and shoulders for women, beards for adult men. Ship Captain and Sailors might wear the same color tunic. Whale wears a whale head and body covering.

(LIGHTS UP FULL ON JONAH entering from left, crossing to center stage, holding a parchment scroll. NINEVITE #1 enters from right crossing to left and is hailed by Jonah.)

JONAH: Say there, citizen of Nineveh, how about buying a copy of my new book?

(Ninevite #1 passes by wordlessly and exits left.)

JONAH: Not much intellectual curiosity in this town!

(NINEVITE #2 enters from left crossing to right and is hailed by Jonah.)

JONAH: Good morning, citizen! How would you like a copy of my new best-selling book?
NINEVITE #2: *(stops)* What's it called?
JONAH: *I Spent Three Days in a Whale Stomach and Lived to Tell about It.*
NINEVITE #2: *(recoils)* Sounds revolting! *(covers mouth, exits right)*
JONAH: It's very exciting! You'd think people here would be grateful for what I did for them. Saved their little town from being wiped off the face of the Earth, is all I did! Oh well, a prophet is never honored in his own land. I forget who said that. Maybe it was me! *(addresses audience)* I'm a prophet, Jonah's the name, how are you today? Say, do you have a minute? Business is slow, let me tell you a story. One day not long ago, I was sitting on a bench in my home village near Nazareth, reading Torah, minding my own business. . .

(LIGHTS FADE DOWN, THEN SPOTLIGHT DOWN LEFT ON Jonah sitting on bench, reading his scroll. A loud voice offstage clears its throat.)

VOICE OF GOD (Offstage): Ahem.

(Jonah continues reading.)

VOICE OF GOD (Offstage): Jonah.

(Jonah looks up briefly, sees no one, returns to reading.)

VOICE OF GOD (Offstage): *(loudly)* Jonah!

(Jonah jumps up, startled, peers around.)

JONAH: Where's that voice coming from? Who's there?

VOICE OF GOD (Offstage): Settle down, Jonah, it's the Voice of God. We need to talk.

JONAH: The Voice of God? I thought You used burning bushes or lightning bolts to get people's attention.

VOICE OF GOD (Offstage): No time for show-and-tell, this is strictly business. Pack your bags, prophet — you're going on a trip to Nineveh.

JONAH: A trip? Nineveh? What? Why? When? Who? Me?

VOICE OF GOD (Offstage): If you don't mind, I'll ask the questions. The people of Nineveh have become very wicked. They have turned away from all that is good and holy. They have lost their faith in God.

JONAH: Nineveh has always been a tough town for God-fearing folk. That's probably why I don't live there. In fact, I don't even want to visit.

VOICE OF GOD (Offstage): You will go to the people of Nineveh and tell them they have forty days to repent of their wickedness.

JONAH: Right, and after they stop laughing and scrape me off the sidewalk—

VOICE OF GOD (Offstage): If they do not repent, I will destroy their city and kill every last person in it.

JONAH: Oh, they'll enjoy hearing that! *(peers around)* Say, is this some kind of gag? Obadiah, are you playing voice tricks on Uncle Jonah again?

(EFFECTS: LIGHTNING FLASH AND THUNDER CRACK; Jonah jumps.)

JONAH: All right, all right, You're serious! But Nineveh is huge! Why, it's the capital of the Assyrian Empire! There must be over a hundred thousand people living there!

VOICE OF GOD (Offstage): One hundred six thousand, three hundred seventy-seven, to be exact. Oops, add two to that total — the queen's serving mistress just had twin girls.
JONAH: One lone prophet is supposed to clean up a town the size of Nineveh?
VOICE OF GOD (Offstage): The Lord your God has spoken! Be on your way!

(Jonah paces.)

JONAH: This is crazy! I'll never be able to persuade everyone in Nineveh to repent and listen to God. They'll laugh me out of the city! And God will get in one of his merciful moods and decide not to destroy them. Then I'll look like a complete moron! "Well, God told me He was going to wipe you wicked Ninevites off the face of the Earth! Of course, He's a busy God, hasn't gotten around to it yet, any day now, you'll be destroyed, don't make plans for next Sabbath." Right! Or worse — they *will* repent, and God *won't* destroy them. And *my* time will have been totally wasted! For this, you need a prophet? I need a vacation!

(LIGHTS UP FULL as Jonah walks toward right and sees a SHIP CAPTAIN and THREE SAILORS at mid right; the Ship Captain stands over the Three Sailors, who are seated on the ground, seated in rowing positions.)

SHIP CAPTAIN: Welcome to Jaffa, the prime port of Phoenicia! We Phoenicians sail all over the known world. You look like you could use a nice refreshing sea voyage.
JONAH: Where is this ship headed?
SHIP CAPTAIN: Tarshish in far away Spain.
JONAH: That's the other side of the Mediterranean from Nineveh, isn't it?

SHIP CAPTAIN: It certainly is, a thousand miles to the west by the Pillars of Hercules.

JONAH: *(hands coin to Ship Captain)* Here's my fare! Anchors aweigh!

(Jonah "steps on board" and stands next to Ship Captain behind Three Sailors who commence rowing and chanting in a singsong rhythm. MUSIC: "Row the Galley.")

THREE SAILORS: *(sing)* Row the galley, row! Cross the sea to Tarshish! Row the galley, row!

JONAH: *(stretches, relaxing)* This is lovely weather! Sun is shining, not a cloud in the sky!

SHIP CAPTAIN: *(mimes guiding the tiller)* It's always nice on the big lake this time of year. You just relax and leave the sailing to us.

JONAH: That's a good idea. The last few days have been such a strain, don't get me started.

(Jonah lies down to left of Sailors and goes instantly to sleep.)

THREE SAILORS: *(sing)* Row the galley, row! Cross the sea to Tarshish! Row the galley, row!

(EFFECTS: STORM WIND RISES; Ship Captain and Sailors look nervously up and around.)

SAILOR #1: Captain, there are storm clouds to the west!
SAILOR #2: Storm clouds to the east!
SAILOR #3: North and south, too!
SHIP CAPTAIN: A hurricane is approaching! How can this be?

(EFFECTS: STORM WIND HOWLS; LIGHTNING FLASH AND THUNDER CRACK.)

SHIP CAPTAIN: Faster, row faster!

(Sailors row faster.)

SAILOR #1: The storm follows! We cannot escape!
SAILOR #2: We are cursed! The gods are trying to kill us!
SAILOR #3: I haven't done anything to displease my god. It must be one of your gods trying to kill you!
SHIP CAPTAIN: Somebody's god is angry, and all of us are going to pay with our lives! Who has brought a bad omen to this ship?
SAILOR #1: Don't give me the evil eye! My god is a very gentle tree in the forests of Lebanon!
SAILOR #2: My god doesn't do violent storms! He only produces earthquakes and volcanoes!
SAILOR #3: What about the passenger we took on at Jaffa? Maybe his god is angry at him?

(Ship Captain rouses Jonah.)

JONAH: Are we there yet?
SHIP CAPTAIN: How can you sleep through such a storm as this? Call on your god for help, or we will all die!

(EFFECTS: LIGHTNING FLASH AND THUNDER CRACK; Jonah leaps to his feet.)

JONAH: I was afraid this might happen, but that's the way the prophet bounces.
SHIP CAPTAIN: What are you babbling about? Pray to your god to save us!
JONAH: I don't think my God wants to hear from me right now. He sent me on a mission, and I have refused to carry it out. This storm is His retribution!

(EFFECTS: LIGHTNING FLASH AND THUNDER CRACK.)

SHIP CAPTAIN: Sorry to hear that! But because you're on our ship, we have to suffer along with you? That hardly seems fair!

JONAH: Indeed. Throw me into the sea, and it will appease my God and save your lives.

(Sailors rise, grab Jonah.)

SAILOR #1: Sounds good to me!
SAILOR #2: This should lighten our load!
SAILOR #3: Hold on. This is a very serious thing we are about to do, sacrificing an innocent man for our sakes. Let us all pray to this man's god and ask to be forgiven for what we are about to do.

(Sailors bow heads.)

SAILOR #1: Everybody sorry?
SAILOR #2: I am.
SAILOR #3: Me, too.
SAILORS #1, #2 & #3: Prophet overboard!

(Sailors begin to heave Jonah toward mid center.)

SHIP CAPTAIN: *(produces coin)* Would you like a refund on your fare?
JONAH: I don't think I'll need it where I'm going, thanks.
SAILORS #1, #2 & #3: Heave away!

(Sailors toss Jonah overboard, and he rolls to mid center, flailing his arms and legs to stay afloat; Sailors and Ship Captain exit right.)

JONAH: Oh, this is wet! And cold! Very wet and very cold! Why does the sea have to be so wet and so cold and glubbbb — so glubbbb — going under!

(LIGHTS OUT; STORM NOISES FADE AND CEASE; a few seconds pass in silence.)

JONAH: So this is what death feels like. Total darkness. Not a breath of air. Absolutely silent.

(SPOTLIGHT ON Jonah sitting at down center.)

WHALE: Shalom, Jonah.
JONAH: Shalom. Who said that?

(SPOTLIGHT INCREASES TO INCLUDE WHALE, who stands a couple feet to Jonah's right.)

WHALE: Welcome to my humble abode.
JONAH: Where am I?
WHALE: You're inside of me.
JONAH: You? What are you?
WHALE: A whale. Huge. Blue. Wet on the outside. Very hungry on the inside.
JONAH: Hold on. If I'm *inside* of you, why am I standing here and you standing there?
WHALE: Because I'm the spirit of the whale talking to you through your unconscious mind.
JONAH: And that's why you look like my Aunt Beryl?
WHALE: Being a spirit without a body, I can look like whatever you wish.
JONAH: In other words, I'm crazy and making this all up.
WHALE: Not at all. Your conscious mind is numb with fear and terror, so your body is asleep. But your unconscious mind is awake and working very hard to figure things out.
JONAH: My luck is getting worse. I'm swallowed by a whale who looks like my least favorite relative and is now talking to me even though we're not really here. Worse yet, this is starting to make sense.

WHALE: Not for long. My whale stomach will start digesting you soon, and you'll be devoured in tiny kelp-size pieces.
JONAH: Any ideas on how I can avoid being dinner?
WHALE: You could ask God for a second chance.
JONAH: Ha! That's a laugh! He's the one who got me here in the first place.
WHALE: Really? I thought you were here because you tried to avoid carrying out what He asked you to do.
JONAH: When I need your opinion, you can ask me for it! Second chance from God! Oh, I forgot, probably *your* last contact with God was during the Great Flood when He decided to spare Noah's family and two of every animal. Nice guy, *that* God. Well, the God we have these days is a pretty different kettle of fish. He's strong! Vengeful! Wipes out whole cities with a single blow! Turns people into pillars of salt! Doesn't take "no" for an answer!
WHALE: It's your choice. But if I were you — and I must say, as a member of the higher order of mammals, I'm glad I'm *not* — but if I *were* a prophet sitting in a dark, slimy whale stomach about to be masticated down to minnow-pulp, I'd give the second-chance-from-God option a shot. After all, He could have already drowned you or had you eaten by a shark; instead He gave you the chance to make another decision. Not bad for a "vengeful" God. *(exits left)*
JONAH: *(on his knees)* Almighty God, you cast me into the deep, into the heart of the seas. I thought, "I am driven from the sight of the Lord." But You have spared my life, and with the voice of thanksgiving I ask that I be allowed to do Your will. I will go to Nineveh and tell the sinners to repent. Send me a sign, O Lord in heaven, that You have heard my prayer!

(EFFECTS: LOUD RUMBLE AND CREAKING; LIGHTS OUT.)

JONAH: Whoaaaaaa!

(NOISES STOP WITH A LOUD THUMP; LIGHTS UP FULL as Jonah picks himself up from ground.)

JONAH: My God never ceases to amaze me! A second ago I was whale snacks; now I'm in the heart of Nineveh!

(Ninevites #1-3 enter from right; Ninevites #4-6 enter from left; they mix and mingle, laughing hysterically, hitting and shoving each other, shouting in anger.)

JONAH: Oh my! There is major decadence in this town! People here are cruel and violent and without any faith in God at all! This is going to take a lonnnnnng time! Here goes!

(Jonah stops a Ninevite.)

JONAH: People of Nineveh! Your attention, please!

(Ninevites stop and listen.)

JONAH: I am Jonah, a prophet from Israel. My God, our God — the one true almighty God in heaven — has told me to tell you that unless you repent in forty days, your city will be totally destroyed. That's the message, it's straight from God, and please, don't feel as if you have to kill the messenger. But, please, repent!

(A moment of silence as Jonah shields himself and Ninevites look at each other, puzzled.)

NINEVITE #1: A tent? He wants us to pitch a tent? I'm a little hard of hearing.
NINEVITE #2: Repent! We're supposed to repent our sins, change our evil ways, and return to God.

NINEVITE #3: Is that all?

NINEVITE #4: Sounds good to me. I'll repent right this very minute!

NINEVITE #5: Me, too! *(to Ninevite #6)* Say, Assur, you want to come with us and repent?

NINEVITE #6: Definitely! I've been wanting to repent for a long time, just haven't got round to it, so much going on with the family.

(Ninevites #1-3 exit right and Ninevites #4-6 exit left, chatting amiably and praying; Jonah stands at down center, frowning.)

JONAH: That's it? They've forsworn their wicked ways and repented? Just like that! *(snaps fingers)* The city isn't going to be destroyed? God, how could You do this to me? Isn't this what I said was going to happen? What a waste of my time! I'm going to the desert and just dry up and blow away!

(Jonah crosses to down right, sits on the ground and broods.)

JONAH: *(looks up)* Hmmm, that sun is really getting hot. Guess I'll die of sunstroke, but that's still better than being a tool of a God that can't make up His mind from one minute to the next.

(LIGHTS FADE TO THREE-QUARTER; Jonah looks up in surprise.)

JONAH: A tree? A tree has just appeared in the middle of the desert right over my head? God must have sent it! He saw me suffering from the heat and said, "Give the prophet a tree!" Thanks!

(Jonah relaxes, head bowed; LIGHTS FADE UP TO FULL; Jonah stirs uncomfortably.)

JONAH: I don't believe this. The tree is dead. God plants a tree, then next day sends a hideous worm to eat the tree and kill it so I can broil in the sun. What is the point? Please, just kill me and get it over with!

VOICE OF GOD (Offstage): Jonah.

JONAH: Yeeeessss?

VOICE OF GOD (Offstage): I have given my love and attention to the people of Nineveh, indeed, to the people of all cities. And you are angered by the death of a single tree?

JONAH: *(rises)* Yes, I am angry. Angry enough to die!

VOICE OF GOD (Offstage): But you had no part in its planting or growth. Whereas, you helped the people of Nineveh find the path to goodness.

JONAH: They would have found it anyway!

VOICE OF GOD (Offstage): Of that you cannot be sure. Only true repentance appeases God's anger and atones for sin.

JONAH: I'm useless! If I were a real prophet, I'd create miracles. I can't even keep a tree from dying.

VOICE OF GOD (Offstage): You are a messenger of God. By helping the citizens of Nineveh turn away from sin, you have accomplished one of the greatest miracles of all time.

JONAH: You know, You're right. I did do something pretty good. I take it back, I don't want to die! I'm feeling much better about things!

VOICE OF GOD (Offstage): Then, cease your infernal complaining and get back on the road! Tell all corners of the Earth that they may find deliverance from sin with the Lord God of Israel!

JONAH: *(salutes)* Yes, sir!

(Ninevites #1-3, Sea Captain and Three Sailors enter from right; Ninevites #4-6 and Whale enter from left; all

gather at center behind Jonah and sing. MUSIC: "Jonah and the Whale.")

ALL: *(sing)*

In Bible we are told
Of a prophet who was called
To a city that was steeped in awful sin;
And the people in that place
Were devoid of saving grace,
And the prophet was afraid to enter in.

Then this prophet forth was sent,
That old Ninevah might repent,
But instead to Tarshish he set sail;
Oh! the winds began to blow,
Overboard did Jonah go,
And he found a mercy-seat inside the whale.

Over there, over there,
In that land so bright and fair,
He will tell us all about it over there;
On that happy, golden strand,
We'll take Jonah by the hand,
And he'll tell us all about it over there.

In the cold and briny deep,
Tears of grief did Jonah weep,
And the big fish threw him out upon the shore;
Then he gladly went his way,
Preached to Ninevah night and day,
And he did not care to backslide anymore.

Many souls are tossed about
By the whales of fear and doubt,
But God on high will take them by the hand;
If they will His voice obey,

He will save them right away,
And will guide them safely to the promised land.

Over there, over there,
In that land so bright and fair,
He will tell us all about it over there;
On that happy, golden strand,
We'll take Jonah by the hand,
And he'll tell us all about it over there.

(LIGHTS OUT.)

THE END

Row the Galley, Row

© L.E. McCullough 2000

Jonah and the Whale

(traditional, arranged L.E. McCullough)

NOAH'S ARK:
FALSEHOOD AND WICKEDNESS HITCH A RIDE

This tale is from a collection of Talmudic writings called *midrash* — a form of Scriptural interpretation that uses legends, parables, allegories and proverbs to explore a well-known Bible story, and to delve more deeply into the many meanings of the story. A tale such as Noah's Ark told in the Book of Genesis may have meaning for us in our daily lives. Some *midrashim* provide insight into serious matters of doctrine; others, like this humorous allegory, use symbolism and talking animals to communicate truths about human nature.

STAGE SET: At mid center a platform approximately 8' x 8' at the back edge of which stands a painted flat or scrim depicting The Ark

CAST: 13 actors, minimum 1 boy (•), 1 girl (+)

- Noah
  Falsehood
  2 Bears
  2 Monkeys
  Teacher

+ Noah's Wife
  Wickedness
  2 Deer
  2 Lions

EFFECTS: Sound — wind and rain noise

PROPS: Bible; contract; quill pen; ancient coins; deck chair; glass of lemonade

COSTUMES: Teacher wears modern clothes. Noah, Noah's Wife, Falsehood, and Wickedness wear basic Biblical attire — long-sleeved, plain-colored tunics (ankle-length for females, knee-length for males), sandals, a simple cloth or scarf wrapped around the head and shoulders for Noah's Wife. Animals wear appropriate animal costumes/accessories — headpieces, antlers, manes, tails, paws and claws, and so forth.

(LIGHTS UP RIGHT ON TEACHER *standing at down right thumbing through a Bible; Teacher addresses audience.*)

TEACHER: So you think you know everything about the Bible? Sometimes a lot more happened between the lines and behind the scenes. Take the story of Noah's Ark. Everybody's heard how God chose Noah to build an ark that would save the righteous few from being drowned in the Great Flood — the Flood that was supposed to cleanse the world of evil. Now, we know there still is evil in the world today. Did you ever wonder how it managed to survive all that water?

(LIGHTS OUT RIGHT; LIGHTS UP CENTER AND LEFT where NOAH and MRS. NOAH stand at mid center helping animals enter the Ark; TWO BEARS lumber in from left.)

NOAH: Ohhh, look at that sky! There is going to be a big storm before long!
MRS. NOAH: Come on, you Bears! There is no time to lose!
BEAR #1: All right, Mrs. Noah. Keep your fur on!
BEAR #2: Is there going to be any honey on this trip? I only travel on ships with first-class honey.
MRS. NOAH: Enough chatter! Get aboard quickly!
NOAH: Two by two now, two by two.

(The Bears board the Ark, going behind the flat/scrim; TWO DEER, TWO MONKEYS, and TWO LIONS enter from left and board the Ark; FALSEHOOD enters from left and crosses to down center, pacing nervously.)

FALSEHOOD: This is just awful! The world is coming to an end and I — Falsehood — am going to lose all my customers! The wicked will be drowned, and the righteous, well, what good are they to a liar like me?

(Falsehood runs up to the Ark, cutting in line.)

FALSEHOOD: Please, you have got to let me on board the Ark! I must have sanctuary!
MRS. NOAH: Who is this? What is your name?
FALSEHOOD: Umm, I am one of your grandchildren.
MRS. NOAH: Grandchild? I have never seen you before.

FALSEHOOD: I am from very far away. Wisconsin. No, Luxembourg, that's it. Maybe Nigeria?
LION #1: Hey, who's the lion cutter? Get it — "lion cutter"?
LION #2: Back of the line, pal, and wait your turn!
FALSEHOOD: You have to let me on! Please!
NOAH: I do not recognize you. In any case, you can only come aboard if you have a mate or partner. That is God's rule. I am sorry.

(Falsehood walks dejectedly back to down center as the other animals board the Ark and go behind flat/scrim; WICKEDNESS strolls in from left and watches Falsehood.)

FALSEHOOD: *He's* sorry? *I* am the one going to be eating saltwater taffy for breakfast, lunch, and dinner! Hmmm. . . I know! I will say I am the Ark Inspector, and I have to take a look inside. That's the ticket! Permits, anyone?
WICKEDNESS: *(taps Falsehood on shoulder)* You know, friend, there is an easier way.
FALSEHOOD: *(turns)* What? Oh, it's you, Wickedness.
WICKEDNESS: Guilty as charged. Gee, times are sure tough when a liar like you is forced to tell the truth.
FALSEHOOD: Can you believe it? I can't get on the Ark because I do not have a partner!
WICKEDNESS: You could *pretend* you had one.
FALSEHOOD: Great idea, but who would want to be *my* partner? I am a liar. A thief. A vile, pathetic — hold on? *(points to Wickedness)* You?
WICKEDNESS: And moi? Partners?
FALSEHOOD: It's a lie.
WICKEDNESS: Has that ever stopped you before?
FALSEHOOD: No, siree! *(offers handshake)*
WICKEDNESS: *(turns handshake aside)* Not so fast, friend. What will you give me if I agree to be your partner?
FALSEHOOD: Give you? How about a life where you can breathe oxygen instead of bubbles?

WICKEDNESS: *(turns away)* No can do.
FALSEHOOD: Are you crazy? If you don't become my partner and get on that Ark, you will die!
WICKEDNESS: Eh? Life on this planet is so overrated. Besides, I think I will enjoy the peace and quiet.

(SOUND EFFECT: Thunder crackling and wind rising.)

FALSEHOOD: All right, I will give you everything I earn from my falsehood.
WICKEDNESS: Everything?
FALSEHOOD: Everything! Come on, we have no time to lose!
WICKEDNESS: You are not telling a lie?
FALSEHOOD: No! I will give you everything I earn if you will just be my partner and get on the Ark!

(Wickedness whips out a contract and quill pen.)

WICKEDNESS: Excellent. I happen to have a brief contract handy. Sign at the dotted line, please.

(Falsehood signs, grabs Wickedness by the arm, and marches to the Ark where the Lions have just boarded.)

FALSEHOOD: Here we are, the two of us! Partners! Mates! Amigos for life!
MRS. NOAH: Something does not seem right about this.
NOAH: We have to go by the rules, wife. If there are indeed two of them, they can come aboard.
FALSEHOOD: Yes!!!
MRS. NOAH: Hurry then and get below!

(SOUND EFFECT: Thunder crackling and wind rising; Falsehood and Wickedness step onto the platform, jostling each other; LIGHTS OUT.)

TEACHER: As you might expect, it wasn't any time at all before Falsehood went to work spreading lies and making trouble from one end of the Ark to the other.

(LIGHTS UP CENTER; Deer #1 and Deer #2 stand at front of the Ark.)

DEER #1: *(to Deer #2)* The Monkey said *what?*
DEER #2: I didn't believe it myself! And about the Lion, no less!
DEER #1: That's just terrible!

(Lion #1 and Lion #2 come roaring out from behind flat/scrim.)

LION #1: Where's that loudmouth Bear? I'll show him he can't say that about a member of the feline family!
LION #2: That goes double for me, too!

(Monkey #1 and Monkey #2 spring out from behind flat/scrim.)

MONKEY #1: Over here, Lions! I saw the Bear go over here!
MONKEY #2: Why ever are you looking for the Bear? I thought Lions were frightened of Bears?

(Lions roar and chase Monkeys back behind flat/scrim; Bear #1 and Bear #2 enter from the other side of the flat/scrim and address the Deer.)

BEAR #1: So what's this we hear about a certain pair of Deer —
BEAR #2: Which would be you!
BEAR #1: Saying unkind remarks about a certain pair of Bears —
BEAR #2: Which would be us!

(Deer look at each other, then point to each other.)

Noah's Ark: Falsehood and Wickedness Hitch a Ride

DEER #1: It was him!
DEER #2: It was her!

(Deer scramble back behind flat/scrim followed by lumbering Bears; LIGHTS UP LEFT ON Wickedness lounging in a deck chair at down left, sipping from a tall glass of lemonade; Falsehood enters from left and gives Wickedness a handful of coins.)

FALSEHOOD: There you go!
WICKEDNESS: Business is booming! Excellent work, Falsehood!
FALSEHOOD: Thank you. *(clears throat)* Which brings up a point—
WICKEDNESS: Yes?
FALSEHOOD: I seem to be doing all the work of making mischief, and you get all the profit.
WICKEDNESS: Yes!
FALSEHOOD: If you don't mind me saying so, that hardly seems fair.
WICKEDNESS: I don't mind at all. Keep working, and pretty soon we'll be fabulously rich!
FALSEHOOD: You mean, *you* will be fabulously rich.
WICKEDNESS: Of course!
FALSEHOOD: But *I* do all the work!
WICKEDNESS: Because *you* did all the contract signing when we came on board. Remember?
FALSEHOOD: You won't let me forget.

(Noah and Noah's Wife enter from behind flat/scrim and stand on the platform, peering out toward audience.)

NOAH'S WIFE: The rain has stopped, and the waters are receding.
NOAH: Is that a mountain top I see?
NOAH'S WIFE: Here comes the Dove — she has a fresh-plucked olive leaf in her beak!

NOAH: Dry land! The Dove has found dry land! God has returned life to the Earth! Praise be to His Holy Name!

(All the Animals enter from behind flat/scrim and gather around Noah and Noah's Wife rejoicing and cavorting happily.)

WICKEDNESS: Sounds like the cruise is over. And I was having so much fun!
FALSEHOOD: Me, too. Wait a minute, when we get back on land, I can start working for myself again.
WICKEDNESS: *(displays contract)* Is that a fact? I don't see any end date in this contract. You — Falsehood — will continue to give me — Wickedness — everything you earn, every last bit, forever and ever.

(Falsehood curls fists.)

FALSEHOOD: I have a mind to—
WICKEDNESS: Stop whining! If you have any complaints about our bargain, why don't you just talk to God? *(mimes talking into phone)* "Hello, God speaking? What? You're not receiving ample payment for your evil deeds? I'll get on it right away!" *(chuckles)*

(Falsehood stomps offstage left as Wickedness laughs and plays with coins; LIGHTS FADE DOWN CENTER AND LEFT; LIGHTS FADE UP RIGHT ON Teacher at down right.)

TEACHER: That is one story about Noah's Ark you might not have heard before. Did it really happen? Well, neither you nor I were there, so we can't be completely sure. But here is one thing for certain — whatever Falsehood gains, Wickedness is sure to take away.

(LIGHTS OUT.)

THE END

DARE TO BE A DANIEL!

The story of the prophet Daniel (6th century B.C.E.) is a stirring tale of bravery and courage in the face of ignorance and persecution. While Daniel and his friends Shadrach, Meshach, and Abednego could have easily avoided royal wrath by choosing to renounce their belief in one God, they stood firmly by their principles even to the point of certain death. The song "Dare to Be a Daniel" was written in 1873 by Philip Paul Bliss, a Sunday School teacher in Chicago. Even in modern times Daniel's story still has the power to provoke fear in the hearts of tyrants. The religious songwriter Ira Sankey reported that in the early 1900s, the Sultan of Turkey prohibited the singing of "Dare to Be a Daniel" by any subject of his empire.

STAGE SET: 3 midsized 8' x 8' platforms — one at mid right, one at mid center, one at mid left; a throne sits on platform at mid center

CAST: 21 actors, minimum 8 boys (•)

- Daniel
- Shadrach
- Meshach
- Abednego
- King Darius
  2 Persian Prefects

- King Nebuchadnezzar
- Ashpenaz, Palace Master
- Arioch, Executioner
  2 Babylonian Magicians
  3 Lions
  6 Palace Chorus

EFFECTS: Sound — fire noise

MUSIC: "Battle Fanfare," "Dare to Be a Daniel," "Court Fanfare"

PROPS: 2 short swords; 1 long sword; large golden statue of an idol; wooden cart; royal seal stamp; parchment scroll; fiery furnace (painted shower curtain on a frame or flat wheeled onstage, approximately 6' x 6', tall and wide enough for Shadrach, Meshach, and Abedngeo to go behind and stay unseen)

COSTUMES: Characters wear basic Biblical attire — long-sleeved, plain-colored tunics (ankle-length for females, knee-length for males), sandals, beards for adult men. King Nebuchadnezzar and King Darius wear more brightly colored, richly patterned tunics as well as crowns and other royal accessories. 2 Persian Prefects can wear tapered, light-fitting trousers that were in use among Persian soldiers at the time. Ashpenaz and Arioch can wear Babylonian-style conical hats. Lions wear beige-brown body coverings, manes, paws, tails, and masks.

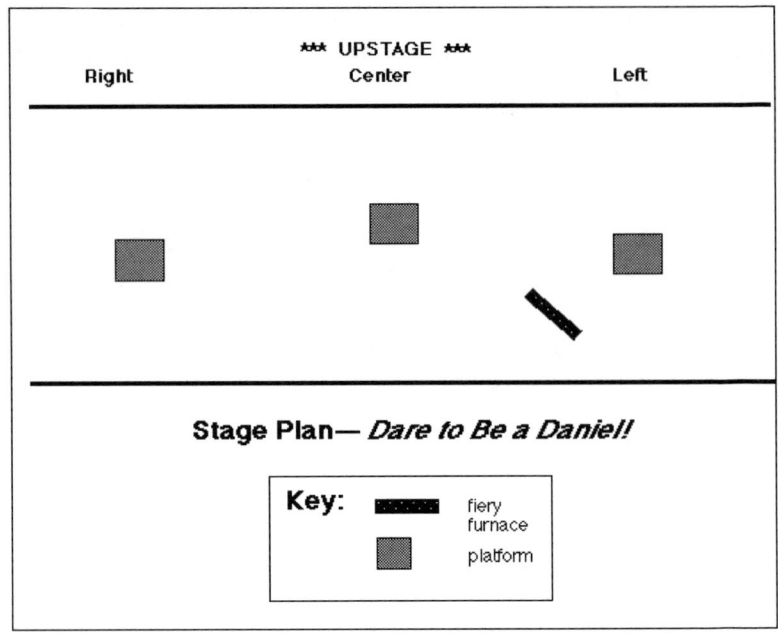

(LIGHTS UP HALF; SPOTLIGHT ON PALACE CHORUS #1-3 standing on platform at mid left; KING NEBUCHADNEZZAR enters from right followed by ASHPENAZ; both wield short swords and attack FOUR ISRAELITES who have entered, weaponless, from left.)

PALACE CHORUS #1: In the third year of the reign of King Jehoiakim of Judah, King Nebuchadnezzar of Babylon came to Jerusalem and besieged it.

(MUSIC: "Battle Fanfare" plays as Four Israelites resist but are beaten down and captured by Nebuchadnezzar and Ashpenaz; Nebuchadnezzar crosses to sit on throne at mid center as Ashpenaz stands Four Israelites in a line at down center facing audience; SPOTLIGHT ON PALACE CHORUS #4-6 standing on platform at mid right.)

PALACE CHORUS #4: Although the Babylonians worshiped many gods, the Lord God of Israel let the Israelites fall into Nebuchadnezzar's power, and Jerusalem was conquered.

PALACE CHORUS #2: Then Nebuchadnezzar commanded his palace master Ashpenaz to bring some young Israelites of the royal family to Babylon.

(SPOTLIGHTS OUT, LIGHTS UP FULL; Ashpenaz brings Four Israelites to throne.)

PALACE CHORUS #5: They were to learn the literature and language of Babylon and be taught to serve in the king's palace.

PALACE CHORUS #3: Among the youths were Daniel—

(Ashpenaz prompts Daniel to kneel before Nebuchadnezzar; Daniel kneels.)

PALACE CHORUS #6: Hananiah—

(Ashpenaz prompts Hananiah to kneel before Nebuchadnezzar; Hananiah kneels.)

PALACE CHORUS #1: Mishael—

(Ashpenaz prompts Mishael to kneel before Nebuchadnezzar; Mishael kneels.)

PALACE CHORUS #4: And Azariah.

(Ashpenaz prompts Azariah to kneel before Nebuchadnezzar; Azariah kneels.)

PALACE CHORUS #2: And the palace master gave them Babylonian names—

(Ashpenaz uses his sword to tap the head of each Israelite as he calls out his new name.)

ASHPENAZ: *(taps Hananiah)* Shadrach! *(taps Mishael)* Meshach! *(taps Azariah)* Abednego! *(taps Daniel)* Belteshazzar!
PALACE CHORUS #5: Which meant — "God preserves his life."
PALACE CHORUS #3: The young Israelites prospered and became favorites of the court.
PALACE CHORUS #6: In every manner of wisdom, Nebuchadnezzar found them ten times wiser than all the magicians and enchanters in the kingdom.

(Nebuchadnezzar blesses Daniel, Shadrach, Meshach, and Abednego; they rise, bow to Nebuchadnezzar and exit right followed by Ashpenaz as LIGHTS FADE DOWN TO HALF. PALACE CHORUS SINGS: "Dare to Be a Daniel.")

PALACE CHORUS: *(sings)*
Standing by a purpose true,
Heeding God's command,
Honor them, the faithful few!
All hail to Daniel's band!

(LIGHTS FADE UP TO FULL AS TWO BABYLONIAN MAGICIANS enter from left, cross to throne and bow before Nebuchadnezzar, who is asleep.)

PALACE CHORUS #1: In the second year of his reign, Nebuchadnezzar dreamed such a dream that his spirit was greatly troubled.

(Nebuchadnezzar wakes with a violent start.)

NEBUCHADNEZZAR: Magicians! Where are the court magicians?

MAGICIAN #1: Here, your majesty! Tell us this dream that troubles you!

MAGICIAN #2: And we will reveal the meaning!

NEBUCHADNEZZAR: *(stands)* No! You must tell me the dream and then its meaning. If you do, you will receive gifts and great honors. If you do not, you shall be torn limb from limb.

MAGICIAN #1: Tell the meaning of a dream without knowing the dream? No king has ever asked this of his magicians!

MAGICIAN #2: There is not a magician or wise man in the kingdom who can do such a thing!

NEBUCHADNEZZAR: Then I, Nebuchadnezzar King of Babylon, decree that all magicians and wise men in the kingdom be put to death! Executioner! Bring me Arioch, my executioner!

(ARIOCH enters from left carrying a long sword; he crosses to down center and faces audience, sword at the ready, as the Two Magicians kneel and cower in fear; Daniel enters from right and stands at down right.)

PALACE CHORUS #4: When Daniel heard of the king's decree, he prayed to the God of the Israelites.

DANIEL: Blessed be the name of God from age to age, for wisdom and power are His. He changes times and seasons, deposes kings and sets up kings; He gives wisdom to the wise and knowledge to those who have understanding. He reveals deep and hidden things; He knows what is in the darkness, and light dwells with Him.

PALACE CHORUS #2: And God revealed the mystery of the king's dream to Daniel.

PALACE CHORUS #5: Whereupon Daniel went to the king.

(Daniel crosses to mid center as Arioch prepares to execute Magician #1; Daniel addresses Nebuchadnezzar.)

DANIEL: O king, do not destroy the wise men of Babylon! I can tell your dream and its meaning!

NEBUCHADNEZZAR: *(to Arioch)* Stay!

(Arioch stays the blow to Magician #1.)

NEBUCHADNEZZAR: *(to Daniel)* You are one of the exiled Israelites, are you not? And you claim knowledge that not even the wisest of our magicians possess?

DANIEL: There is a God in heaven who is the source of all mystery, and He has disclosed through a dream to King Nebuchadnezzar what will happen at the end of days.

NEBUCHADNEZZAR: Continue.

DANIEL: The king saw a great statue, towering high into the air. The head was of fine gold, the chest and arms of silver, the middle and thighs of bronze. The legs of the statue were of iron—

NEBUCHADNEZZAR: And its feet?

DANIEL: Were made partly of iron and partly of clay. As you gazed upon this mighty figure, a stone appeared — as if held by other than human hands — and it struck the statue on its feet of iron and clay and broke them into pieces. Then the rest of the statue was broken, and the pieces became like chaff of wheat. The wind carried them all away so not a trace could be found.

NEBUCHADNEZZAR: But the stone?

DANIEL: The stone that struck the statue became a great mountain, and it grew and grew until it filled the whole Earth.

NEBUCHADNEZZAR: That was my dream! And now the meaning?

DANIEL: You, O king of kings — to whom the God of heaven has given power, might, and glory — you are the head of gold. After you shall arise another kingdom inferior to yours—

NEBUCHADNEZZAR: The chest and arms of silver!

DANIEL: And then a third kingdom of bronze and yet a fourth kingdom strong as iron that shall crush and shatter all these. As the feet were partly of iron and partly of clay, it shall be a divided kingdom with strength and weakness mixed. But the God of heaven — like the stone in your dream — shall make a kingdom that will crush all others and stand forever.

(Nebuchadnezzar kneels with arms outstretched before Daniel.)

NEBUCHADNEZZAR: Truly your God is God of all gods and Lord of all kings!

(Two Magicians and Arioch exit left; Daniel exits right; Nebuchadnezzar sits on throne; PALACE CHORUS SINGS: "Dare to Be a Daniel.")

PALACE CHORUS: *(sings)*
　Dare to be a Daniel,
　Dare to stand alone!
　Dare to have a purpose firm,
　And dare to make it known!

(Ashpenaz enters from right pushing a cart that holds a large golden statue of an idol; he stops the cart at the right of the throne.)

PALACE CHORUS #3: Though Daniel had won respect by interpreting the king's dream, Nebuchadnezzar would not give up the worship of idols.

PALACE CHORUS #6: The king ordered a statue of a golden idol to be made and placed where it could be worshiped by everyone in the kingdom.

ASHPENAZ: When the horn and pipe and drum sound the call, anyone who does not fall down and worship, shall immediately be thrown into a furnace of blazing fire!

(Two Magicians enter from left and approach the throne, bowing.)

MAGICIAN #1: O wondrous king, you are the light of Babylon, the most powerful monarch in the world!

MAGICIAN #2: But there are some who dispute your authority.

NEBUCHADNEZZAR: My authority?

MAGICIAN #1: Certain Israelites — Shadrach, Meshach, Abednego — pay no heed to you. They will not worship your golden idol.

NEBUCHADNEZZAR: Is this true!?

ASHPENAZ: I will call them to court, your majesty. You may ask them yourself.

(MUSIC: "Court Fanfare" plays as Shadrach, Meshach, and Abednego enter from right and cross to down center.)

NEBUCHADNEZZAR: The call to worship has sounded. All must kneel and worship the golden idol.

(Ashpenaz and Two Magicians bow before idol; Shadrach, Meshach, and Abednego remain standing.)

NEBUCHADNEZZAR: Why do you not obey the king's command to worship?

SHADRACH: We mean no disrespect to your gods, O king.

MESHACH: But our God, the one God in heaven, commands us to worship none but Him.

NEBUCHADNEZZAR: *(rises)* Then you shall be thrown into the fiery furnace!

ABEDNEGO: Our God whom we serve will deliver us from the blazing fire.

NEBUCHADNEZZAR: Into the furnace! Make it seven times hotter than before!

(Arioch enters from left pushing a fiery furnace to down left, where it is set at a 45° angle to the stage front; Two Magicians prod Shadrach, Meshach, and Abednego to furnace; Daniel enters from right and stands at down right watching.)

NEBUCHADNEZZAR: Into the fire! Let your one God in heaven save you now!

(SOUND: FIRE NOISE as Two Magicians push Shadrach, Meshach, and Abednego into furnace [they step to left behind flat and wait]; Two Magicians and Arioch begin to shout and contort in pain.)

MAGICIAN #1: The flames! They are leaping higher!
ARIOCH: The furnace is too hot!
MAGICIAN #2: I am on fire! Aauugghh!

(Two Magicians and Arioch scream and fall to floor and die; fire noise fades.)

DANIEL: Shadrach, Meshach, and Abednego — servants of the Most High God — come out from the furnace!

(Shadrach, Meshach, and Abednego come out right from behind furnace and stand at down center facing audience.)

ASHPENAZ: Not a hair of their heads has been singed! Not a stitch of their tunics has been harmed! Not even the breath of fire fills the air around them!

DANIEL: They yielded their bodies to the care of our Lord. He did not forsake them.

NEBUCHADNEZZAR: Truly your God is God of all gods and Lord of all kings! I decree from this hour henceforth that any people, nation, or language that utters blasphemy against the God of the Israelites shall be torn limb from limb!

(Nebuchadnezzar and Ashpenaz exit left, removing fiery furnace; Shadrach, Meshach, and Abednego exit right; KING DARIUS enters from left and sits on throne; he is followed by TWO PERSIAN PREFECTS who stand on either side of his throne and stare at Daniel who stands with hands folded in prayer at down right; PALACE CHORUS SINGS: "Dare to Be a Daniel.")

PALACE CHORUS: *(sings)*
    Many giants, great and tall,
    Stalking through the land,
    Headlong to the earth would fall,
    When met by Daniel's band.

PALACE CHORUS #1: And the time came when the Empire of Babylon fell to King Darius of Persia, who formed the greatest kingdom ever known to man.

PALACE CHORUS #4: Darius gave Daniel charge of his accounts, and many in the court became jealous of the Israelite's power.

PREFECT #1: King Darius, you are the most exalted ruler on Earth!

PREFECT #2: All the prefects agree that you should establish a law to befit your status.

KING DARIUS: What sort of law?

PREFECT #1: That for thirty days whoever shall pray to

anyone — divine or human — other than you, shall be thrown into a den of lions.

KING DARIUS: That seems like a reasonable law.

PREFECT #2: Then sign it with your royal seal.

(Prefect #1 holds a parchment scroll and Prefect #2 gives Darius a royal seal stamp, with which he stamps the parchment.)

KING DARIUS: It is done!

(Daniel kneels and prays.)

PALACE CHORUS #2: Even though Daniel knew of the law, he continued to go to his own house and pray three times a day, his face turned toward Jerusalem.

PALACE CHORUS #5: The prefects from court spied upon him and reported to Darius.

(Prefects point at Daniel.)

PREFECT #1: O mighty king! Daniel, one of the exiles from Israel, defies your law of worship!

PREFECT #2: He prays to his God in Jerusalem three times a day!

KING DARIUS: And how many times to me?

PREFECTS #1 & #2: None!

KING DARIUS: I see. But Daniel is one of my most trusted servants. We shall let this pass.

PREFECT #1: Your majesty, by the law of the Medes and Persians, we cannot let it pass!

PREFECT #2: Once a king has established a law, it cannot be changed. Even by the king!

KING DARIUS: *(sighs)* Bring Daniel to me.

(Prefects grab Daniel and prod him to the throne; Daniel bows.)

Dare to Be a Daniel!

DANIEL: I am yours to command, my King.

KING DARIUS: You have been commanded to worship no one — divine or human — besides me, for thirty days. Yet you continue to worship the God of Israel?

DANIEL: He is the one God in heaven.

KING DARIUS: Then I have no choice but to carry out the sentence of the law you have broken. May your God, whom you so faithfully serve, deliver you. Take him to the lions' den!

(Prefects prod Daniel to down left; THREE LIONS enter snarling from left; LIGHTS FADE TO HALF; Prefects give Daniel a shove toward Lions, who circle warily around him; Prefects scurry back to throne and stand on either side of Darius.)

DANIEL: Incline your ear, O my God, and hear the plea of your servant! You who have brought Your people out of Egypt and made Your name renowned among the nations of the world, rescue us from this exile!

(PALACE CHORUS SINGS: "Dare to Be a Daniel.")

PALACE CHORUS: *(sings)*
Dare to be a Daniel,
Dare to stand alone!
Dare to have a purpose firm,
And dare to make it known!

(SPOTLIGHT ON Daniel and Lions; while Palace Chorus sings, Daniel stands with hands folded in prayer facing audience; Lions snarl and circle, then become quiet and lie down at his feet; MUSIC ENDS; LIGHTS FADE UP TO FULL.)

KING DARIUS: *(pointing)* Daniel lives!
PREFECT #1: The lions have not touched him!
PREFECT #2: How is this possible?

(Daniel steps away from the Lions and crosses to down center.)

DANIEL: My God shut the lions' mouths because I was blameless before Him, and blameless before you, my King.

KING DARIUS: I decree that everyone in my kingdom tremble and pray before the God of Daniel!

(Prefects kneel.)

DANIEL: For He is the living God enduring forever. His kingdom shall never be destroyed, and His dominion has no end. He delivers and rescues, works signs and wonders in heaven and on earth. He is the God of Israel, the God of all humankind.

(PALACE CHORUS SINGS: "Dare to Be a Daniel.")

PALACE CHORUS: *(sings)*
Hold the Bible banner high!
On to vict'ry grand!
Satan and his hosts defy,
And shout for Daniel's band.

Dare to be a Daniel,
Dare to stand alone!
Dare to have a purpose firm,
And dare to make it known!

(LIGHTS OUT.)

THE END

Battle Fanfare

© L.E. McCullough 2000

Court Fanfare

© L.E. McCullough 2000

Dare to Be a Daniel

(words & music by Philip Paul Bliss, arranged L.E. McCullough)

RUTH AND NAOMI: THE HEALING POWER OF FRIENDSHIP

In this popular Bible tale frequently read during Shavuot (Festival of Weeks), the names of the main characters give a clue as to the roles they play. In Hebrew, Naomi means "sweetness" and Ruth means "friendship." The two sons of Naomi who die in their youthful prime are Mahlon ("sickness") and Chillion ("wasting away"). Orpah, whose loyalty to her in-laws is weak, means "back of the neck" — which is what one sees when a supposed friend leaves at a critical moment. And Boaz means "fleetness" — a fitting epithet for a man who quickly responded to the opportunity God placed in his path. The story of Ruth and Naomi has much to say about perseverance, about trust, about welcoming newcomers to the fold, about a community pulling together to help its less fortunate members. Other legends attach to this tale: According to one, Orpah was the great-great-grandmother of Goliath. And the marriage of Ruth and Boaz established the line of descent that would later produce King David. Coincidence? Or divine destiny?

STAGE SET: A rock or boulder at down left large enough to sit on

CAST: 10 actors, minimum 1 boy (•), 3 girls (+)
+ Ruth   + Naomi
+ Orpah   • Boaz
  3 Reapers   3 Israelites

MUSIC: "Eli Tziyon," "Le-Hayim!"

PROPS: Burlap bag; 3 scythes or simple 2-prong rakes; a bowl of barley

COSTUMES: All characters wear basic Biblical attire — long-sleeved, plain-colored tunics (ankle-length for females, knee-length for males), sandals, a simple cloth or scarf wrapped around the head and shoulders for the women, beards for adult men. Boaz wears a more colorful tunic befitting his greater wealth. Ruth, Naomi, and Orpah each wear a black sash or headband denoting recent widowhood.

GLOSSARY: *Ha-zot Naomi?* — Is this Naomi?

(LIGHTS UP CENTER ON RUTH and ORPAH standing on either side of NAOMI at down center. They look out at audience. Naomi is older than the two other women and appears somewhat weak, occasionally leaning on Ruth and Orpah for support. They sing; MUSIC: "Eli Tziyon.")

NAOMI, RUTH, & ORPAH: *(sing)*
  Eli Tziyon veareha
  Kemo ishah betzireha
  Vekhiv'tulah haguratsak
  Aley vaal neureha

Ruth and Naomi: The Healing Power of Friendship

I sing of Zion among her cities
Like a woman caught in birth-pangs
And like a maiden dressed in sackcloth
In mourning for the husband of her youth

ORPAH: It will be a long trek to Israel through the burning desert.
RUTH: The journey will be a test of our faith, my sister.
ORPAH: Faith! I fear my faith died with my husband Chillion. Are you not afraid of leaving Moab, Ruth? It has been your home since birth.
RUTH: When I married Mahlon, I learned of another home where everlasting joy resides.
ORPAH: And where will you find this joy, now that he, too, lies dead of the sickness?
NAOMI: Orpah and Ruth, calm yourselves. The things of this world may come and go. My husband, Elimelech, is dead, and so are both my sons — your husbands — who have left you without child. I must return to Israel, the land of my birth. You two should stay in Moab and return to your families.
RUTH: No, we will come with you, Naomi!
NAOMI: Why? I have no more sons to become your husbands! Turn back now!

(Naomi begins to walk slowly toward right, and Ruth follows; Orpah hesitates and does not follow but takes a step backward.)

ORPAH: Ruth! Stay with me here in Moab! We will not be welcome in a foreign land!
NAOMI: Go! I am old, and you owe me nothing! Go back with Orpah!

(Ruth rushes to Naomi, stops her, and kneels at her feet.)

RUTH: Do not press me to leave you. Where you go, I will go. Your people shall be my people. Your God shall be my God.

(Naomi does not reply but pats Ruth gently on the head, once, then turns and continues walking right, exiting right.)

RUTH: Orpah, come with us to Israel. We will find joy there together. Naomi's God is a god of goodness and bounty.
ORPAH: If this God that Naomi worships is a good God, He would not have taken our husbands!
RUTH: He will give us even greater blessings in the days to come!
ORPAH: I do not share your faith, Ruth. Farewell, my sister.

(Orpah exits left as Ruth hurries offstage right to catch up with Naomi.)

(LIGHTS OUT FOR A FEW SECONDS, THEN UP FULL ON THREE ISRAELITES STANDING AT DOWN LEFT AROUND A BOULDER; they watch as Ruth helps Naomi enter from right and cross to center.)

ISRAELITE #1: Hazot Naomi? Naomi, wife of Elimelech?
ISRAELITE #2: She left Israel for Moab ten years ago! How greatly she has aged!
ISRAELITE #3: Who is that foreign woman with her?
ISRAELITE #1: I do not know, but she wears the scarf of a widow.
ISRAELITE #2: What a shame a young woman like her must be without a husband!
ISRAELITE #3: Here come Boaz and his reapers. He is a kinsman of Naomi and very wealthy.

Ruth and Naomi: The Healing Power of Friendship

(BOAZ AND THREE REAPERS ENTER FROM LEFT; they stop and greet Naomi and Ruth at down center [Reapers carry scythes and/or rakes].)

BOAZ: Welcome to Israel, Naomi. We are glad you have returned.

NAOMI: I am pleased to be again in the land of one God. This is my daughter-in-law, Ruth. She is a Moabite.

(Ruth bows before Boaz).

BOAZ: All are welcome in the land of Israel. Our God has provided us with great bounty.

NAOMI: Boaz is my cousin, and he has promised to let us live on his land.

RUTH: We do not want charity. I can work. Please, permit me to follow your reapers as they thresh grain in the fields. Whatever I pick up from their leavings will be our sustenance.

BOAZ: As you wish. *(to Reaper #1)* Give this woman a sack for her gleaning.

(Reaper #1 gives Ruth a burlap bag; Reapers move to down right and begin reaping grain, with Ruth standing behind and picking up bits of grain from ground and putting them in the bag; Boaz helps Naomi to boulder, where Three Israelites help her sit and rest; then Boaz crosses to mid center where he watches Ruth as she gleans.)

ISRAELITE #1: Boaz has long sought a wife to head his household.

ISRAELITE #2: He is a generous man, but cautious.

ISRAELITE #3: Perhaps he worries that the fate which befell the husbands of Ruth and Naomi might befall him?

(The Reapers exit right as Ruth continues to glean; Boaz crosses to down right.)

BOAZ: You have worked hard in the fields today. If you wish, you may come to my table and eat your supper.

RUTH: Why should I find favor in your sight? I am but a foreigner.

BOAZ: All that you have done for your mother-in-law has been told to me. Here, do not go back to her empty-handed. Take these extra six measures of barley and give them to Naomi. *(hands Ruth a bowl of barley)*

(Ruth bows and crosses to Naomi sitting on rock at left and gives her the bowl; Three Israelites have moved to mid center.)

NAOMI: Blessed be the one who has taken notice of you! You must anoint yourself and prepare for the assembly of my people.

(Boaz crosses to down center and addresses the Three Israelites.)

BOAZ: Elders of the city, I wish to acquire the hand of Ruth the Moabite in marriage.

ISRAELITE #1: We are witnesses to your deed.

ISRAELITE #2: By doing so you will preserve the inheritance of Naomi.

ISRAELITE #3: And bring into your house a woman who will build up the house of Israel.

(Boaz crosses to down left and removes the black band of mourning from Ruth's head.)

ISRAELITE #1: The Lord will give Ruth and Boaz many children.

ISRAELITE #2: They will have a child renowned throughout Israel.

ISRAELITE #3: He will be a mighty warrior and great king who leads his people to victory.

NAOMI: Blessed be the Lord of Israel who forsakes neither the living or the dead!

(All characters sing; MUSIC: "Le-Hayim!")

ALL: *(sing)*
    Le-hayim tovim uleshalom!
    Le-hayim tovim uleshalom!

    To a good life and to peace
    And praise to the Lord our God!
    Le-hayim tovim uleshalom!

(LIGHTS OUT.)

THE END

Eli Tziyon

(trad., arr. L.E. McCullough)

Ruth and Naomi: The Healing Power of Friendship

Le-Hayim!

(trad., arr L.E. McCullough)

SAMSON AND DELILAH

The tale of mighty Samson and treacherous Delilah has been celebrated in story and song for centuries as a caution against straying from commitment to a faith-based way of life. For the people of ancient Israel, this was certainly an important theme as they struggled to cope with idol-worshipping overlords such as the Philistines. In the United States during the late 1800s and early 1900s, the tale caught the fancy of many religious songwriters, and several songs called "Samson and Delilah" can be found in the Library of Congress Folk Song Archive. The rendition by Rev. Gary Davis (1896–1972), a singing preacher in New York City, was perhaps the most popular.

The text of this play can be recited in a basic rhyming cadence, or it can be sung to the melody of the verse as shown in the musical examples. Listen to a recording of the song* to get a feel for the word-flow. If you have a flexible pianist or guitar player, give the singing version a try. Or be very brave and try it *a cappella* — with just voices!

* The original version by Rev. Gary Davis can be heard on *Rev. Gary Davis and Pink Anderson: Gospel, Blues and Street Songs* (Riverside RLP-148). More recent versions include recordings by guitarist Ernie Hawkins of Pittsburgh (http://www.erniehawkins.com) on the CD *Blues Advice* or guitarist Andy Cohen of Memphis (rivnrev@memphisonline.com) on his CD *Oh Glory, How Happy I Am: The Sacred Songs of Rev. Gary Davis*.

STAGE SET: A temple altar at mid center — 2 marble pillars to the right of a large altar stone, with several other pillars and smaller blocks resembling a temple edifice (cardboard boxes or styrofoam pieces painted to resemble stone and marble)

CAST: 21 actors, minimum 2 boys (•), 2 girls (+)

•	Samson	+ Delilah
	Lion	+ Samson's Mother
	Angel	6 Philistine Soldiers
•	Philistine Lord	4 Philistine Temple-goers
	Teacher	4 Children

MUSIC: "Samson and Delilah"

EFFECTS: Sound — rumbling earthquake; a stone building crashing to the ground (offstage tape)

PROPS: Jawbone of an ass; spears and swords for Soldiers; stool; sacrificial bowl

COSTUMES: Teacher and Children wear contemporary clothes. Bible characters wear basic Biblical attire — long-sleeved, plain-colored tunics (ankle-length for females, knee-length for males), sandals, a simple cloth or scarf wrapped around the head and shoulders for Samson's Mother, beards for adult men, with Samson needing a long-haired wig that can be removed when his locks are shorn. Delilah wears a gown-like costume with excessive jewelry. Philistine Lord wears brightly colored, richly patterned tunic, a crown, and other royal accessories. Soldiers wear armor, helmets, and leather leggings. Lion wears beige-brown body coverings, mane, paws, tail, and mask.

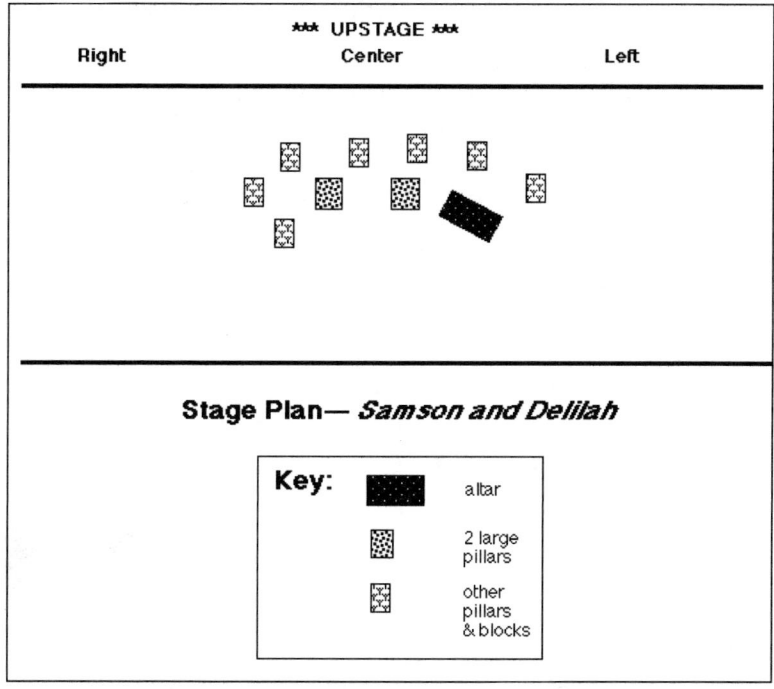

Stage Plan— *Samson and Delilah*

(LIGHTS UP RIGHT ON TEACHER standing at down right and strumming a guitar, facing an audience of FOUR CHILDREN grouped in a semicircle.)

TEACHER: Who wants to hear a Bible story?
FOUR CHILDREN: We do!
TEACHER: This is a Bible story you can sing along with. It's in Judges Thirteen to Sixteen, and it happened in Israel a long, long time ago — when a man named Samson met a woman named Delilah. And they made Bible history!

(MUSIC: "Samson and Delilah.")

TEACHER: *(sings)*
If I had my way,
If I had my way,
If I had my way,
I would tear this old building down!

TEACHER: That's the chorus of the song! You try it!
TEACHER: *(sings)* If I had my way,
FOUR CHILDREN: *(sing)* If I had my way,
TEACHER: *(sings)* If I had my way,
FOUR CHILDREN: *(sing)* I would tear this old building down!
TEACHER: That's good! And that's what Samson sang when he was being mocked by the Philistines! But the story starts way before that. *(stops playing guitar)* It starts with an angel of God appearing before Samson's mother.

(LIGHTS OUT RIGHT; LIGHTS UP LEFT ON SAMSON'S MOTHER standing at down left, miming sowing seeds in a field; ANGEL enters from left and stands behind her.)

TEACHER:
Now, Samson's mother was a hardworking woman;
She sowed in the fields all day.
Didn't matter whether rain or shine,
She would always kneel to pray.

(Samson's Mother kneels and prays.)

SAMSON'S MOTHER:
All these years I've waited for a child
To raise up as my own,
But the Lord must have some other plans
For I'm barren as a bed of stone.

(Angel steps forward, touches her shoulder.)

ANGEL:
The Lord above has heard your plea
And listened to your prayer.

Because of your abiding faith,
A child you'll shortly bear.

Do not consume any fruit of the vine
Or eat of food unclean;
For this child to do the work of God
He must be strong and lean.

And once the child begins to grow,
His scalp must never be shorn.
He must always proudly wear his locks,
Despite how others scorn.

(LIGHTS OUT LEFT; LIGHTS UP RIGHT on Teacher and Four Children singing at down right; MUSIC: "Samson and Delilah.")

TEACHER & FOUR CHILDREN: *(sing)*
If I had my way,
If I had my way,
If I had my way,
I would tear this old building down!

(LIGHTS OUT RIGHT; LIGHTS UP LEFT ON SAMSON standing at down left.)

TEACHER:
Well, a boy was born to her,
And Samson was his name.
He grew up to be a man
Of mighty strength and fame.

He became the leader
Of the Israelite clan,
Who were kept as lowly servants
In the Philistine land.

(Samson's Mother enters from left; he takes her arm and they cross to down center.)

TEACHER:
>One day while he was walking
>With his aged mother dear,
>Down to the town of Timnah
>To try and bring her cheer.

(LION enters from left and stalks Samson and Samson's Mother.)

LION: Roar!

(Samson gets his Mother behind him and faces the Lion bare-handed.)

SAMSON:
>Hey there, Mister Lion,
>You better not attack!
>Cause if you do, I'll punish you
>And dance upon your back!

LION:
>I've never met a human
>Who could match me in the dirt.
>I'll have you for my dinner
>And your mother for dessert!

(Samson and Lion grapple.)

SAMSON'S MOTHER:
>You hear about this lion
>Had killed so many with his paws!
>But Samson got his hand
>In that lion's dripping jaws!

(Lion dies, with Samson astride his body.)

SAMSON'S MOTHER:
    He rid that beast and rid him
    Until he killed him dead,
    And the bees they made their honey
    In the lion's sorry head!

(LIGHTS OUT LEFT; LIGHTS UP RIGHT on Teacher and Four Children singing at down right; MUSIC: "Samson and Delilah.")

TEACHER & FOUR CHILDREN: *(sing)*
    If I had my way,
    If I had my way,
    If I had my way,
    I would tear this old building down!

(LIGHTS OUT RIGHT; LIGHTS UP LEFT ON SAMSON standing at down center.)

TEACHER:
    Now Samson was a thorn
    In the Philistines' side.
    He stood up for his people
    And defended their pride.

(SIX PHILISTINE SOLDIERS enter from left and prepare to attack Samson.)

TEACHER:
    The Philistines got angry
    A thousand men the king did send
    To capture mighty Samson,
    Put his freedom to an end.

(Samson reaches to the ground and picks up the jawbone of an ass.)

SAMSON:
    What is this before me?
    A thousand men seek me to slay?
    With this donkey's humble jawbone
    I'll praise the Lord today!

(Six Philistine Soldiers attack Samson and are easily dispatched by his jawbone, as they fall and stumble offstage left followed by a victorious Samson.)

(LIGHTS OUT LEFT; LIGHTS UP RIGHT on Teacher and Four Children singing at down right; MUSIC: "Samson and Delilah.")

TEACHER & FOUR CHILDREN: *(sing)*
    If I had my way,
    If I had my way,
    If I had my way,
    I would tear this old building down!

(LIGHTS OUT RIGHT; LIGHTS UP LEFT ON SAMSON standing at down center, PHILISTINE LORD and DELILAH stand at down left and conspire.)

TEACHER:
    Samson could not be taken
    By any soldier in the land.
    But he had a fatal weakness
    That he never could withstand.

(Delilah crosses to Samson, walks by him, and gets his attention.)

PHILISTINE LORD:
   Delilah is a woman
   With beauty fair and fine.
   She'll find out Samson's secret
   And vengeance will be mine!

(Philistine Soldier #1 enters from left carrying a stool, which he hands to Philistine Lord, who places it down left as Delilah begins to weave around Samson; Philistine Lord moves to edge of curtain, as if eavesdropping.)

DELILAH:
   Tell me, mighty Samson,
   Where does your great strength lie?

SAMSON:
   That is a holy secret
   Between my Lord and I.

DELILAH:
   You tell me that you love me,
   But I don't believe it's true.

SAMSON:
   What can I say, Delilah,
   To prove my love to you?

DELILAH:
   Samson, Samson, tell me,
   Where does your great strength lie?
   If you want to marry me,
   I need a quick reply.

SAMSON:
   My strength lies in the lengthy locks
   That proudly crown my head.
   They never can be shaven
   Or my power will be shed.

(Delilah leads Samson to stool; she sits, and he lays his head on her lap.)

DELILAH:
Rest yourself, dear Samson,
Don't you fuss or fret.
Your secret's surely safe with me,
Your trust you won't regret.

(Philistine Lord waves a Philistine Soldier #2 onstage as Samson falls asleep on Delilah's lap; Delilah addresses Philistine Lord.)

DELILAH:
Bring your sword and shave his head,
Shave it clean as my hand,
And watch as Samson's strength becomes
Natural as any other man.

(Philistine Soldier #2 uses a short sword to cut off Samson's hair.)

DELILAH: *(speaks)*
Samson! Samson! The Philistines are upon thee!

(Samson awakes as other five Philistine Soldiers rush in from left; Samson struggles briefly but is easily subdued.)

SAMSON:
Strength has departed from me,
Since I betrayed my Lord.
No rescue I deserve,
No mercy I implore.

(Philistine Soldier #3 takes sword and blinds Samson.)

PHILISTINE LORD:
He stands weak as a puppy

And gentle as a lamb.
Take him down to Gaza
He can push the grinding ram.

(LIGHTS OUT LEFT; LIGHTS UP RIGHT on Teacher and Four Children singing at down right; MUSIC: "Samson and Delilah.")

TEACHER & FOUR CHILDREN: *(sing)*
If I had my way,
If I had my way,
If I had my way,
I would tear this old building down!

(LIGHTS OUT RIGHT; LIGHTS UP CENTER ON SAMSON kneeling at mid center in front of the altar, head bowed; Six Philistine Soldiers stand behind him at attention; FOUR PHILISTINE TEMPLE-GOERS sit on ground to left and right of mid center, pointing and laughing at Samson.)

TEMPLE-GOER #1: There's the mighty man of Israel!
TEMPLE-GOER #2: Look at him scrape and bow!
TEMPLE-GOER #3: He's not so big and fearsome!
TEMPLE-GOER #4: Why, he couldn't hurt a cow!

(Philistine Lord enters from left accompanied by Delilah; he carries a sacrificial bowl, and they cross to mid center, where Philistine Lord stands in front of altar and addresses assembly.)

PHILISTINE LORD:
It is time we make an offering
To our idols bold and grand
For delivering this noble enemy
Into our waiting hands.

DELILAH:
>   My heart weeps for his suffering
>   And the shame his people bear.
>
>   But, mark, his locks have thickened;
>   Will he yet escape this snare?
>
>   *(Delilah folds her hands in prayer; Samson stands and reaches out his arms.)*

SAMSON:
>   Suffer me to feel the pillars
>   Whereupon this house does stand,
>   And I will show the wrath of God
>   Spares no woman, child, or man.
>
>   *(Delilah moves Samson to a spot between the two main pillars and places his arms on the pillars as Temple-goers and Soldiers laugh and mock, and Philistine Lord places sacrificial bowl on altar and begins to pray over it.)*

TEMPLE-GOER #1: Oh, spare us, spare us, Samson!
TEMPLE-GOER #2: Your words have turned us pale!
TEMPLE-GOER #3: I suppose you'll come attack us—
TEMPLE-GOER #4: With the jawbone of a snail!

>   *(Temple-goers and Soldiers laugh as Samson digs in on the pillars with all his strength.)*

SAMSON:
>   Lord God, oh, please remember me
>   Do not desert your servant yet!!
>   Let me teach these idol lovers
>   A lesson they won't forget!
>
>   *(The two main pillars begin to move and buckle. SOUND: rumbling earthquake. Temple-goers and*

Soldiers cease laughing as SOUND increases. MUSIC: "Samson and Delilah.")

TEACHER & FOUR CHILDREN: *(sing)*
If I had my way,
If I had my way,
If I had my way,
I would tear this old building down!

PHILISTINE LORD:
The temple crashes down upon our heads!
Stop him quick or we'll all be dead!

(Pillars and blocks tumble to the floor as Temple-goers and Soldiers flail and fall to the ground. SOUND: a stone building crashing to the ground.)

DELILAH:
For our treachery and pride we now will pay!
Samson's God has won the day!

(Delilah and Philistine Lord fall to ground as Samson staggers to his knees and looks up to heaven.)

SAMSON: *(speaks)*
You have forgiven me, O Lord! Now let me die with the Philistines, for we are all the same in Your eyes — sinners in need of Your salvation!

(Samson collapses. MUSIC: "Samson and Delilah.")

TEACHER & FOUR CHILDREN: *(sing)*
If I had my way,
If I had my way,
If I had my way,
I would tear this old building down!

If I had my way
If I had my way
If I had my way
I would tear this old building down

(LIGHTS OUT.)

THE END

Samson and Delilah

(traditional, arranged L.E. McCullough)

76 Plays of Ancient Israel

Samson and Delilah, pg. 2

~ All verses continue in same pattern of 8 measures per rhymed couplet. Melody and rhythm can be adjusted to the words of each verse . ~

TALES OF ANGELS

Angels appear frequently in the Bible, performing a wide variety of functions that include delivering important messages from God and aiding humans in battle and other extreme emergencies. Many angel legends come from the Midrash, the collections of Scriptural commentary made by Jewish scholars over the last fifteen hundred years. There are two types of Midrash commentaries — the Midrash Halacha, which focus on Jewish religious law — and the Midrash Aggada, which comprise philosophy and folklore. Closely related to the topic of angels is the Midrash Aggada legend of the Lamed Vav, the thirty-six "hidden saints," whose good works keep the world balanced in times of peril. Elements of the Lamed Vav story appear in many modern versions, such as the 1997 Hollywood film *Men in Black* and the 1895 short story by I.L. Pertez "Bontshe Shvayg."

STAGE SET: A city park with a park bench at down right, a small table with two chairs at mid center, a basketball hoop at mid left

CAST: 21 actors, minimum 6 boys (•), 3 girls (+)
+ Judy (age 8-10)
• Zeke (age 8-10)
Angel Michael
Angel Gabriel
Angel Metatron
Angel Raphael
Angel Uriel
Angel Sammael

+ 2 Girls Skipping Rope
2 Elderly People Playing Chess
2 Kids Playing Basketball
2 Lions
• Abraham
• Isaac
• Daniel
Angel Sandalfon
Angel Akatriel

EFFECTS: Sound — thunder and lightning or discordant music announcing entrance of Angel Sammael

PROPS: Bible; large knife; chess set

COSTUMES: Judy, Zeke, Kids Playing Basketball, Elderly People Playing Chess and Girls Skipping Rope wear contemporary clothes. Abraham, Isaac and Daniel wear basic Biblical attire — plain-colored, ankle-length tunics, sandals, optional beards. Lions wear beige-brown body coverings, manes, paws, tails, and masks. Angels wear long robes of various luminescent or bright-effect colors (gold, silver, teal, lavender, rose, perhaps black for Angel Sammael) with squared shoulders that emphasize height and power. Halos and wings are optional.

(LIGHTS UP RIGHT ON JUDY *sitting on park bench at down right, reading the Bible.* ZEKE *enters from right and approaches her, shuffling with his hands in his pockets; he is frowning and ill at ease.*)

JUDY: Hi, Zeke! How are you?
ZEKE: Oh, hi, Judy. Guess I'm okay. What about you?
JUDY: I'm terrific! It's a beautiful day to be in the park.
ZEKE: Yeh, guess so.
JUDY: Say, are you really okay? You look a little down.
ZEKE: Not as down as I'm going to be. I've got a math test this afternoon, and it's going to be ugly.
JUDY: Haven't you studied?
ZEKE: Sure, harder than ever, but I just know I'm going to mess up. I need a miracle to pass!
JUDY: *(displays Bible)* Miracles have been known to happen.
ZEKE: Oh, yeh, in the Bible thousands of years ago. But do you think some angel is going to swoop down and give me the right answers *today*? Like an angel has nothing better to do than watch school kids taking math tests!
JUDY: You might be surprised at what angels can do.
ZEKE: Really? Okay, talk to me about angels.
JUDY: Well, the first thing you have to know about angels is their main purpose is to serve God. But they serve humans, too, in all kinds of ways. Angels have appeared to us as guardians, guides, counselors, judges, matchmakers, interpreters. They've helped find lost articles, increase wealth, strengthen faith, introduce plagues, and destroy enemies.
ZEKE: Yeh! Maybe an angel can send a plague of mice into school today! Or at least knock out the electricity for a few hours!
JUDY: Sorry, Zeke, but angels generally do positive things — calming storms, feeding hermits, converting heathens, helping farmers, carrying saints to heaven, turning the tide of battle.

ZEKE: Anything in there about boosting math test scores?
JUDY: Angels are the instruments by which God communicates divine will to humans. The Hebrew word for angel is *malach*, which means *messenger*. And that's mostly what they did in the Tanakh, or Old Testament — convey messages from God.
ZEKE: Oh, like the time when Abraham was about to kill Isaac!

(LIGHTS UP LEFT ON ISAAC KNEELING AT DOWN LEFT, HANDS TIED BEHIND HIM; ABRAHAM STANDS OVER HIM WITH A KNIFE UPRAISED.)

ABRAHAM: The Lord God of Israel has commanded me to make a burnt offering. And it is my only son, Isaac, who must be sacrificed.

(Abraham prepares to stab Isaac as ANGEL MICHAEL ENTERS FROM LEFT.)

ANGEL MICHAEL: Stay your hand, Abraham, and do not harm the boy!

(Abraham and Isaac shrink from Angel Michael.)

ISAAC: It is an angel, father!
ANGEL MICHAEL: I am the Angel Michael, servant of the Lord. Now that God knows you are willing to sacrifice your only son, He will bless you and make your offspring as numerous as the stars of heaven and the sand upon the shore.

(LIGHTS OUT LEFT.)

ZEKE: Way cool!

JUDY: Michael is one of seven archangels who reside closest to God. His name in Hebrew means "he who is like God."

ZEKE: And then there's, what's-his-name, Gabriel that plays the trumpet?

JUDY: Gabriel's name means "strength of God." No one knows how he became associated with a trumpet. Except it might have something to do with his main job, which is to dispense divine justice and punish the wicked. It was Gabriel who commanded the destruction of Sodom and Gomorrah.

ZEKE: Awesome!

JUDY: But he also saved lives. He kept Shadrach, Meshach, and Abednego from being burned in the fiery furnace of Babylon. And when Daniel was thrown into the lions' den—

(LIGHTS UP LEFT ON DANIEL SITTING AT DOWN LEFT, HEAD BOWED AND HANDS OUTSTRETCHED; TWO LIONS CIRCLE MENACINGLY AROUND HIM, GROWLING.)

DANIEL: Incline your ear, O my God, and hear the plea of Your servant! You who have brought Your people out of Egypt and made Your name renowned among the nations of the world, rescue us from this exile!

(ANGEL GABRIEL ENTERS FROM LEFT.)

ANGEL GABRIEL: Because of your faithful service to the living God, I — the Angel Gabriel — have been sent to deliver you!

(Angel Gabriel shuts the mouths of the Two Lions, who lie down and become meek; Daniel stands.)

DANIEL: For the God of Israel is the living God! He delivers and works signs and wonders in heaven and on Earth!

(LIGHTS OUT LEFT.)

ZEKE: That was amazing! How many angels are there?
JUDY: Thousands, millions, it's impossible to count them all. The Bible and the Midrash — which are Jewish legends that further explain stories in the Bible — mention lots of angels. Some of the main ones besides Michael and Gabriel are Raphael—

(LIGHTS UP LEFT AS ANGEL RAPHAEL, ANGEL URIEL, ANGEL METATRON, ANGEL SANDALFON, AND ANGEL AKATRIEL ENTER FROM LEFT AND STAND IN A SEMICIRCLE FACING AUDIENCE.)

ANGEL RAPHAEL: *(steps forward)* My name is Raphael, which means "God has healed." I guided Tobias to Nineveh, healed the wound on Jacob's leg and gave Noah a book of cures for humankind after the Great Flood.
ANGEL URIEL: *(steps forward)* My name is Uriel, which means "splendor of God." I was sent to warn Noah of the flood, led Abraham out of Ur, and helped bury Adam and Abel in Paradise.
ANGEL METATRON: *(steps forward)* My name is Metatron, which means "teacher of teachers." I am responsible for keeping order in the world and was the pillar of fire and cloud who helped the Hebrews cross the Red Sea from Egypt.
ANGEL SANDALFON: *(steps forward)* My name is Sandalfon, which means "twin brother," for I am the twin brother of Metatron. I take the prayers of humanity and weave them into heavenly crowns.

ANGEL AKATRIEL: *(steps forward)* My name is Akatriel, which means "lord of hosts." I stay close to humans in order to hear their deepest thoughts and then relay these to God.

(SOUND EFFECT: THUNDER AND LIGHTNING, OR DISCORDANT OFFSTAGE MUSIC; LIGHTS FLICKER OFF AND ON AS ANGEL SAMMAEL ENTERS FROM LEFT.)

ANGEL SAMMAEL: And I am the Angel Sammael! Which translates as "poisonous angel"! You may know me better by some of my other names — Satan, Lucifer, Prince of Darkness. Doesn't matter what you call me, I keep very busy in the affairs of humankind. I refused to recognize God as the Supreme Being, and for that trifling offense, was banished from heaven for all eternity. Say, anyone here want to wreak some misery and death?

(Other Angels forcibly shove Angel Sammael offstage left; LIGHTS OUT LEFT.)

ZEKE: With Sammael on the loose, we sure need lots of good angels!
JUDY: That's where the legend of the *guardian angel* comes in. When a person is born, they receive their own angel especially commissioned to guard and assist them. Remember Psalm 90 where it says, "For God has given His angels charge over you; to keep you in all your ways."?
ZEKE: I wonder if my guardian angel ever took algebra before?
JUDY: I don't think it works that way, Zeke. And besides, angels aren't what really determines how things happen here on Earth. It's the Lamed Vav.
ZEKE: The what?

JUDY: The Lamed Vav. *Lamed* and *vav* are the third and sixth letters of the Hebrew alphabet. Put them together and they form the number *thirty-six*.

ZEKE: I'm with you so far.

JUDY: Legend says that the world has to have exactly thirty-six righteous people in each generation. These are people who are good and kind, selfless and honest.

ZEKE: Sure, but why these special thirty-six, these Lamed Vav?

JUDY: Well, most days God looks out on the world, and He gets very depressed. He sees all the greed and meanness and selfishness that human beings commit, and He says to himself, "All right, that's it, I've had enough! This experiment has failed! I'm going to dump the whole mess."

ZEKE: What stops Him?

JUDY: Only one thing — the fact that at any one moment, somewhere on Earth, there are thirty-six good people, the Lamed Vav.

ZEKE: So who are these Lamed Vavniks? Is it the President? A bunch of billionaires? Some movie stars?

(LIGHTS FADE UP LEFT AND CENTER AS SEVERAL CHARACTERS ENTER FROM LEFT — TWO GIRLS SKIPPING ROPE AT DOWN LEFT, TWO ELDERLY PEOPLE PLAYING CHESS AT MID CENTER TABLE, TWO KIDS PLAYING BASKETBALL AT MID LEFT.)

JUDY: Not at all. The Lamed Vav are "hidden saints." No one knows who they are, because they're just ordinary people. They're not rich or famous or powerful in any earthly way.

ZEKE: They could be anybody? Anybody at all?

(Judy points to 2 Elderly People Playing Chess.)

Tales of Angels 85

JUDY: It could be those two old folks sitting under the tree playing chess.

ZEKE: Hmmm, I've seen that one old guy before. Always had my suspicions.

JUDY: Or it could be either of those kids shooting hoops. Or one or both of those girls playing jump rope.

ZEKE: Or the guy bagging groceries at the supermarket.

JUDY: *(points to audience)* Or the woman waiting at the bus stop over there.

ZEKE: *(points to audience)* Or the school crossing guard.

JUDY: *(points to audience)* Or the homeless man collecting soft drink cans on the corner.

ZEKE: Or somebody you never even know, like an accountant in Nebraska.

JUDY: A farmer in Bangladesh.

ZEKE: A truck driver in Beijing.

JUDY: Maybe even your math teacher.

ZEKE: No way! Okay, I get it. You never know who might be one of the thirty-six people in charge of keeping the world safe, so anyone could be a Lamed Vavnik.

JUDY: There's one more thing. Not even the Lamed Vav know who they are.

ZEKE: What?

JUDY: And when one dies, he or she has to be replaced right away to keep the balance of thirty-six.

ZEKE: That's crazy! I mean, I'd be a Lamed Vav, it sounds like fun. But how can you apply if you don't know who the others are?

JUDY: Gosh, Zeke, how do you know you're not a Lamed Vav already?

ZEKE: Huh?

(LIGHTS FADE OUT LEFT AND CENTER; Judy stands and turns to exit right.)

JUDY: The legend says that every time a person has a chance to do a good deed, that might just be our invitation to become one of the Lamed Vav.

ZEKE: Like an audition? Yeh, I see!

JUDY: But if we don't come through, if we don't do the right thing on that day, if we take the shortcut and the easy way out—

ZEKE: The thirty-six could become thirty-five!

JUDY: And at that very moment—

ZEKE: The world would end—

JUDY: Because there wasn't enough goodness left—

ZEKE: To keep God from destroying Creation!

JUDY: Good luck on your math test! *(exits right)*

ZEKE: Math test! Who can think about math when the fate of the world is hanging in the balance! I better find a way to do something good and pronto! *(turns to exit right, stops and faces audience)* Then again, anyone could be the next Lamed Vav. *(points)* Even one of *you*. Better get busy! *(exits)*

(LIGHTS OUT.)

THE END

WHAT IS A BROTHER?

The Bible contains a wealth of stories about family relationships, especially the often fragile bonds between brothers. Typically, these tales of brotherly interaction are filled with strife, deceit, and tragedy. Yet, each story — be it that of Cain and Abel, Jacob and Esau, Joseph and his brothers — offers much wisdom about the nature of love, responsibility, and forgiveness. . . and, as in the tale of Menasseh and Simon, occasionally has a happy ending.

STAGE SET: A living room chair at down right

CAST: 19 actors, minimum 13 boys (•), 5 girls (+)

- + Grandma
- • Benjamin
- • Nathan
- • Jacob
- • Isaac
- • Joseph
- • Judah
- • Levi
- • Menasseh
- Voice of God (Offstage)

- • Cain
- • Abel
- + Eve
- • Esau
- + Rebecca
- + Leah
- • Reuben
- • Simon
- + Shifra

PROPS: Book; video game cartridge; jug of water; pallet; 2 bowls; piece of blanket resembling goatskin covering; sheaf bundle; large basket; pitchfork

COSTUMES: Grandma, Benjamin, and Nathan wear modern clothes. Other characters wear basic Biblical attire — long-sleeved, plain-colored tunics (ankle-length for females, knee-length for males), sandals, a simple cloth or scarf wrapped around the head and shoulders for Eve, Rebecca, Rachel, and Shifra. Joseph has a tunic of many bright colors.

(LIGHTS UP DOWN RIGHT ON GRANDMA sitting in a chair at down right, quietly reading a book; two young boys, BENJAMIN and NATHAN, burst in from right, squabbling over a video game cartridge Nathan carries.)

BENJAMIN: Give it here!

What Is a Brother? 89

NATHAN: No! It's mine! The new Mega 9000 Super Action Killatron is *mine*!
BENJAMIN: Dad bought it for me!
NATHAN: Then play it on your own machine!
BENJAMIN: I can't. It's broken.
NATHAN: Then you can't have it!
GRANDMA: Boys, boys! Quiet down! You know there's no shouting in the house!
BENJAMIN: I'm sorry, Grandma.
NATHAN: Me, too. But Benjamin started it.
BENJAMIN: Did not. Nathan did.
NATHAN: Did so.
BENJAMIN: Did not!
GRANDMA: That's enough! Why can't both of you play with the toy?

(Benjamin and Nathan look sheepishly at each other, shrug.)

GRANDMA: That's better. If someone saw you arguing like that, they'd think you were mortal enemies instead of twin brothers.
NATHAN: But brothers are supposed to fight, aren't they?
GRANDMA: Whatever gave you that silly idea?
BENJAMIN: It's in the Bible, bunches of times. Cain and Abel—
NATHAN: Jacob and Esau—
BENJAMIN: Joseph and his brothers. They all were enemies.
NATHAN: We're just following the Bible, Grandma. It's natural for brothers to hate each other's guts. *(sticks tongue out at Benjamin, who curls a fist)*
GRANDMA: Is that a fact? Why don't you tell me what you *think* you read in the Bible about brothers.
NATHAN: *(to Benjamin)* Okay, you first.
BENJAMIN: No, you.
NATHAN: No, you.

BENJAMIN: No, *you*!
GRANDMA: Boys!
NATHAN: All right, since I'm the oldest twin—
BENJAMIN: By thirteen seconds!

(LIGHTS DOWN RIGHT; LIGHTS UP LEFT ON CAIN and ABEL entering from left.)

NATHAN: After Adam and Eve had been sent forth from the Garden of Eden, they had two sons. One was named Cain, and the other was named Abel. Cain was a tiller of the soil, and Abel kept a herd of livestock.

(EVE enters from left carrying a jug of water.)

EVE: My sons, it is time to bring an offering of our bounty to the Lord God, our Creator. Come, let us go.

(Eve, followed by Cain and Abel, steps forward to the edge of the stage. She lays her jug of water on the ground, bows, and steps back, followed by Cain who mimes laying down a handful of vegetables and Abel who mimes laying down a sheep.)

NATHAN: And the Lord God spoke—
VOICE OF GOD (Offstage): The offering of Abel is pleasing.
ABEL: Thank you, Lord. I shall strive to please you till the end of my days.
CAIN: And, I, Lord? What of my offering? Is it not also pleasing?

(Silence; Cain rises angrily.)

CAIN: But I work just as hard in the fields as my brother!
EVE: Son, calm yourself!
CAIN: Why will you not accept my offering?

VOICE OF GOD (Offstage): If you do well, will your offering not be accepted? If you do not do well, sin is lurking at the door. Its desire is for you, but you must master it.

(Eve exits left, leaving her jug of water; Abel puts his hand consolingly on Cain's shoulder; Cain shakes it off, then smiles at Abel.)

CAIN: Dear brother, let us go out into the field.

(Abel starts toward down center; Cain picks up jug of water, sneaks up behind Abel and slams Abel over the head with the jug; Abel falls; Cain stands triumphant for a moment, then cringes, realizing his deed.)

VOICE OF GOD (Offstage): Cain! Where is your brother, Abel?
CAIN: I do not know! I do not know! Am I my brother's keeper?

(Cain rushes offstage left; LIGHTS DOWN LEFT; LIGHTS UP RIGHT ON Grandma, Nathan, and Benjamin at down right.)

NATHAN: What a great story, huh? Cain just clobbered Abel, and he was outa there!
GRANDMA: Don't forget, Cain lost his power to till the soil, and he became a fugitive and wanderer, cursed into eternity.
NATHAN: Oh. Bummer!
BENJAMIN: The story of Jacob and Esau is even better. Cause the smarter younger brother gets the goods!

(LIGHTS DOWN RIGHT; LIGHTS UP LEFT ON REBECCA helping an ailing ISAAC enter from left; JACOB and ESAU follow behind carrying a pallet they lay on the floor at down left; Rebecca eases Isaac on to the pallet, where he lies on his back.)

BENJAMIN: Their father, Isaac, was very old and coming close to death. It was time for him to give his blessing to the son that would inherit all his wealth — Esau.

(Esau kneels at Isaac's side.)

ISAAC: My first son Esau, holder of my birthright. Take your bow and hunt game for me, then bring it to me to eat so I may bless you before I die.
ESAU: Yes, father.

(Esau rises and exits left as Rebecca takes Jacob aside and whispers to him.)

BENJAMIN: But Isaac did not know that Esau had already sold his birthright to Jacob. Or that the boys' mother, Rebecca, had plans for which brother should receive their father's blessing.
REBECCA: *(to Jacob)* Go to the flock and bring me two young goats that I may prepare a meal for your father.

(Jacob hesitates.)

REBECCA: Hurry!

(Jacob exits left.)

REBECCA: *(to audience)* It has been foretold that Jacob is destined to be the heir of Abraham. I will prepare the meal for Isaac and disguise Jacob as his brother.

(Jacob enters carrying a goatskin covering and a bowl; Rebecca fits the goatskin over his head and upper back.)

REBECCA: Isaac is nearly blind. Take this food to him and let him touch the goatskin. He will think you are Esau.

(Jacob approaches Isaac and lays the bowl at his side as Rebecca hangs back at the edge of the curtain, watching.)

ISAAC: Esau? Is that you?
JACOB: Yes, father, it is I, Esau, your firstborn. I have brought you a meal.
ISAAC: How is it you have found it so quickly?
JACOB: Because the Lord your God granted me success.
ISAAC: Come near that I may touch you to know whether you are Esau.

(Jacob hesitates, looks at Rebecca who encourages him, then leans down to Isaac who touches the goatskin.)

ISAAC: The voice I hear is that of Jacob, but this is the skin of Esau.

(Jacob draws back; Isaac raises his arms.)

ISAAC: I give my blessing to you. May God give you the dew of heaven and the fatness of the earth.

(Isaac lowers his arms; Esau enters from left carrying a bowl.)

ESAU: Father, I have brought you a savory meal. Eat of it and give me your blessing.
REBECCA: It is too late, Esau. Isaac has given his blessing to your brother, Jacob. It is he who will become the heir of Abraham.

(Rebecca, Esau, Jacob, and Isaac freeze in position; LIGHTS DOWN LEFT; LIGHTS UP RIGHT ON Grandma, Nathan, and Benjamin at down right.)

NATHAN: Gosh, do you think Mom would pull a stunt like that?
BENJAMIN: Well, I *am* the smarter younger brother.
NATHAN: So was Joseph. Remember what happened to him?

(LIGHTS DOWN RIGHT; LIGHTS UP LEFT ON JOSEPH sitting contentedly at down left, facing audience; JUDAH, REUBEN, and LEVI stand behind him, huddled together and starting at him; LEAH stands to right arranging a bundle of sheaves.)

NATHAN: After cheating his brother Esau of his birthright and blessing, Jacob went off to another land and had twelve sons. Jacob loved all his sons, but it was for Joseph that he had the most regard. This did not go unnoticed by the other brothers. One day several of them were helping their mother, Leah, gather grain.
JUDAH: Look at our brother Joseph! Silly dreamer does nothing all day, but it is *he* whom our father loves the most!
LEVI: Did you hear the dream he had last night? *(picks up sheaf bundle from Leah)* That *we* were all sheaves in the field, and *our* sheaves were bowing down to *his*?
REUBEN: Does this mean he will reign over us?
LEAH: Your brother has the gift of prophecy. Do not fault him for what God has given.
JUDAH: How can you take his side, when you are our mother and but his stepmother?
LEVI: I have heard enough. Let us go pasture the flock.

(Judah, Reuben, and Levi cross to mid center and sit in a semicircle.)

LEAH: Joseph, your brothers have been gone a long while. Perhaps you should see if all is well with them.
JOSEPH: Yes, Leah.

What Is a Brother? 95

(Leah exits left; Joseph rises and looks around, seeking his brothers.)

JUDAH: Here comes our brother Joseph, the dreamer. Let us kill him and say he was attacked by a wild animal.
LEVI: Then we shall see what becomes of his dreams!
REUBEN: No! Do not kill him! Throw him in this pit!

(Joseph approaches mid center.)

JOSEPH: My brothers, I have had a dream.
JUDAH: Was it this?

(Judah and Levi seize Joseph and throw him down.)

LEVI: *(points offstage left)* Here comes a caravan of Ismaelites. Let us sell our brother to them as a slave!

(Judah, Reuben, and Levi drag Joseph offstage left; LIGHTS DOWN LEFT; LIGHTS UP RIGHT ON Grandma, Nathan, and Benjamin at down right.)

NATHAN: Shows what happens to snotty little brothers.
BENJAMIN: But don't forget — years later, when Joseph was rich and powerful, his brothers came begging his forgiveness. Begging!
GRANDMA: It's wonderful to see you boys take such an interest in Scripture. I think that deserves extra ice cream for dessert tonight!
BENJAMIN & NATHAN: Yay!
GRANDMA: But wait. There's one more brother story, the best brother story of all — the story that shows what being a brother is really all about. Long ago in the land of Israel, there were two brothers named Simon and Menasseh.

(LIGHTS DOWN RIGHT; LIGHTS UP LEFT ON MENASSEH and SHIFRA entering from left, carrying a large basket they set on the floor at down center.)

GRANDMA: Menasseh was married to a wonderful and wise woman named Shifra, who greatly resembled your grandmother in many ways. He had a brother named Simon, who was not married but lived by himself across the field.

(SIMON enters from left carrying a pitchfork; he and Menasseh embrace.)

SIMON: It has been five years since we inherited this farm from our father. We have prospered greatly.
SHIFRA: You have prospered because you share the work equally. There is never a cross word or quarrel between you.
MENASSEH: This year the Lord God has blessed us with a very good harvest.
SIMON: Tomorrow we will take the sheaves and thresh them into grain. Good night, my brother.
MENASSEH: Good night.

(Menasseh and Shifra exit left; Simon crosses to mid center and lies down to sleep.)

GRANDMA: The brothers went home to sleep. But during the night, Simon was unable to sleep, and soon, he woke, and his mind was troubled.

(Simon sits up.)

SIMON: Menasseh and I have always equally shared our labor. But I am not sure that we should take an equal share of the harvest. After all, I am a single man, and my brother has a wife and a growing family. His needs are

What Is a Brother? 97

greater than mine. It would be selfish for me to claim half the harvest.

(Simon rises, taking his pitchfork, and crosses to basket at down center, where he mimes pitching sheaves from the basket into two piles.)

GRANDMA: Simon got up and went to the field. One by one, he took the sheaves from his pile and put half of them into his brother's pile. Then, with a deep feeling of satisfaction, he went back to his home and slept the sleep of the just.

(Simon leaves the pitchfork at down center and crosses to mid center, where he lies down and sleeps; Menasseh enters from left, followed by Shifra.)

GRANDMA: Meanwhile, Menasseh had also had trouble sleeping.
SHIFRA: What is wrong, husband?
MENASSEH: I do not think it is fair to divide the harvest equally between my brother and me. The Lord God willing, our children will take care of you and me in our old age. But Simon will have no one to support him.
SHIFRA: Then go to the field and take some sheaves from our pile and give them to Simon. He will think they are part of his share. *(exits left)*

(Menasseh crosses to down center, where he picks up the pitchfork and mimes pitching sheaves from the basket into two piles.)

GRANDMA: By then, the clouds had covered the moon, and Menasseh could barely see the piles of sheaves. But, one by one, Menasseh took half the sheaves from his pile and put them into his brother's pile. Then, exhausted by his labor, he lay down in the field and slept the sleep of the just.

(Menasseh puts down the pitchfork and lies down to sleep; Simon awakes and crosses to down center.)

GRANDMA: Early the next morning, Simon came to the field and found his brother sleeping beside the piles of sheaves.
SIMON: What is this? Both piles are the same!

(Menasseh awakes.)

MENASSEH: The same? But how can this be?

(Simon and Menasseh look at each other, look at the piles, look at each other, as Shifra enters from left.)

SHIFRA: Do you not see what has happened? During the night each of you came to the field and gave half your share to your brother. Come, let us feast and celebrate God's goodness and bounty.

(Simon, Menasseh, and Shifra happily exit left; LIGHTS DOWN LEFT; LIGHTS UP RIGHT ON Grandma, Nathan, and Benjamin at down right.)

GRANDMA: Now, *there* is a story of what a brother should be.
NATHAN: *(gives cartridge to Benjamin)* Here, Ben, you can play the game.
BENJAMIN: *(refuses cartridge)* Thanks, Natie. But, it's your game, *you* should play it.
NATHAN: *(puts cartridge in Benjamin's hand)* No, really. *You* take it.
BENJAMIN: *(shoves it back at Nathan)* No, I couldn't.

NATHAN: *(shoves it back at Benjamin)* Come on. Take the game.

BENJAMIN: *(shoves it back at Nathan)* You're too kind. But, no!

GRANDMA: Boys! What if you both play at the same time? Does that seem like a good idea?

NATHAN: Gee, Grandma, you sound like our teacher. Always trying to be logical.

BENJAMIN: Yeh, like that other Bible guy, what was his name?

NATHAN: The one that wanted to take his sword and cut somebody's baby in two?

GRANDMA: You're talking about King Solomon. Once upon a time in the land of Israel—

BENJAMIN: That's okay, Grandma, we'll be quiet.

NATHAN: See you at supper.

(Benjamin and Nathan exit right.)

GRANDMA: *(to audience)* Being a grandparent today takes the wisdom of Solomon, the patience of Job, and the bravery of Daniel. And they didn't have to know anything about video games!

(LIGHTS OUT.)

THE END

THE PROPHET AND THE RABBI

Of the many Prophets mentioned in the Bible, Elijah of Gilead is one of the most acclaimed, having performed many miracles before finally being lifted into heaven upon a whirlwind of fiery chariots. Believed to have lived during the eighth century B.C.E., he appears in many forms throughout the ages as a messenger of God, instructing scholars and protecting the poor and weak.

STAGE SET: A stool at down right

CAST: 7 actors, minimum 4 boys (•), 2 girls (+)

- Prophet Elijah
+ Old Woman
  Goat
+ Susanna
- Rabbi Zev
- Old Man
- Merchant

PROPS: Shofar; rag; soup bowl

COSTUMES: All characters wear basic Biblical attire — long-sleeved, plain-colored tunics (ankle-length for females, knee-length for males), sandals, a simple cloth or scarf wrapped around the head and shoulders for Old Woman, beards for adult men. Merchant can have more elaborate accessories, brightly-colored tunic, jewelry. Goat wears goat headpiece or mask, goatskin-like body covering.

GLOSSARY: *bo-ker tov* — good morning; *sho-far* — a musical horn; *to-da* — thank you; *lai-la tov* — good night; *lekh mi-po* — go away; *sha-lom* — hello or good-bye; *she-ket* — silence

(LIGHTS UP RIGHT ON SUSANNA sitting on stool at down right, polishing a shofar with a rag.)

SUSANNA: Boker tov! I am Susanna, daughter of Joab, the shofar maker here in Jerusalem marketplace. I enjoy helping my father with his work, because the shofar is one of the most important musical instruments in all Israel. When it sounds the start of the Sabbath, every ear listens to its plaintive call. And I like watching all the people come and go in the market. Why, just the other day, I saw the prophet Elijah pass by and knock on the door of our neighbor, Rabbi Zev. It is true!

(LIGHTS DOWN RIGHT; LIGHTS UP LEFT ON ELIJAH entering from left; he stands at down left peering around as if seeking someone.)

ELIJAH: Rabbi Zev! Where is the house of Rabbi Zev?

(RABBI ZEV enters from left.)

RABBI ZEV: I am Rabbi Zev. Who is it that seeks me?

ELIJAH: I am the Prophet Elijah. I come in response to your prayers.

RABBI ZEV: Is it truly the great Prophet? Standing in front of me in the plain light of day?

ELIJAH: You prayed often and with great fervor. Almighty God has granted your request.

RABBI ZEV: Yes, yes, I prayed, I fasted, I did many good works! But not for myself, you understand. I asked God to send the Prophet Elijah so that I can learn how to be a better rabbi.

ELIJAH: What do you wish to learn?

RABBI ZEV: Wisdom, Holy One! The wisdom that comes from observing a great teacher, such as yourself.

ELIJAH: Wisdom is not always found where one first looks or in the form one thinks it to be.

RABBI ZEV: If you would allow me to simply follow you as you walk through the world, I would be eternally grateful.

ELIJAH: Agreed. But on one condition.

RABBI ZEV: Yes?

ELIJAH: Under no circumstances may you question my actions. You may learn from observing only.

RABBI ZEV: Whatever you wish, master!

(LIGHTS DOWN LEFT; SPOTLIGHT UP RIGHT ON Susanna at down left.)

SUSANNA: The Prophet set off for the edge of the city, with the rabbi following close behind, observing all that he could. It was very late when they finally stopped — in front of a poor, tumbledown dwelling where an old man and woman lived with their goat.

(SPOTLIGHT OFF; LIGHTS UP CENTER on Elijah and Rabbi Zev standing at down center; at mid center are OLD MAN, OLD WOMAN, and GOAT, lying on the floor, asleep.)

ELIJAH: Call and see if anyone is at home.
RABBI ZEV: Here? Surely you do not want to stop here? There is a comfortable lodging house only a mile up the road. This place, why, it is a hovel!
ELIJAH: We will spend the night in this house.
RABBI ZEV: As you wish, master. Hallo! Hallo, is anyone at home?

(Old Woman awakes, rouses Old Man, who rises and greets the visitors.)

OLD MAN: Welcome, travellers! I see you are hungry and tired. Our house is very humble, but my wife and I can at least provide you with a bowl of soup and a place to sleep.
ELIJAH: Toda. We do not wish to trouble you, only to speak awhile and gain shelter from the night.

(Elijah and Rabbi Zev sit down and are attended to by Old Woman, as Old Man brings forward Goat.)

OLD WOMAN: Come in, come in. *(to Rabbi Zev)* You look famished, rabbi.
RABBI ZEV: It has been a very long time since my last meal.
OLD WOMAN: Have a bowl of soup. *(hands Rabbi Zev a bowl of soup)*

RABBI ZEV: You are most kind. *(eagerly slurps the bowl of soup)*
ELIJAH: That is a fine goat.

(Goat bleats happily.)

OLD MAN: He is the only object of value we have. Once I owned many goats, but this is the last. I hope he can see us through our old age.
ELIJAH: May you and your wife be blessed with long lives in each other's company. Now, we shall rest. Laila tov.
OLD MAN: Laila tov.

(Goat bleats happily, and Old Man and Old Woman lie down on either side of Goat as LIGHTS FADE DOWN CENTER TO HALF.)

SUSANNA: Though he was very tired, the rabbi had great difficulty sleeping. He tossed and turned all night, bedeviled by disturbing dreams. In the morning, he awoke to tragedy.

(LIGHTS UP CENTER on Old Man and Old Woman trying to awaken Goat, as Elijah sits and watches.)

ELIJAH: I am sorry for your loss.
OLD MAN: He seemed perfectly healthy but a few hours ago!
OLD WOMAN: How could he die in the middle of the night? The poor creature!
RABBI ZEV: The goat is dead?
ELIJAH: It is the will of God. Shalom.

(Old Man and Old Woman weep over Goat, as Elijah and Rabbi Zev cross to down left.)

RABBI ZEV: *(to Elijah)* You must have asked God to strike down that goat. Why? What harm did those poor people ever do to you?

ELIJAH: Sheket! Remember your promise — under no circumstances may you question my actions.

(Rabbi Zev starts to protest but stops, sighing.)

RABBI ZEV: Very well, master. Where are we going today?
ELIJAH: Watch. . . and learn.

(LIGHTS OUT as Old Man, Old Woman, and Goat exit, and Elijah and Rabbi Zev cross to down left.)

SUSANNA: The Prophet went back into the city, with the rabbi again following close behind, and again observing all that he could. At nightfall they stopped in front of a great mansion.

(LIGHTS UP LEFT on Elijah and Rabbi Zev facing a MERCHANT standing sternly at down left.)

RABBI ZEV: I must say, this is a far better choice of lodging than before. And here is our host. *(to Merchant)* Greetings, sir. I am Rabbi Zev and this is—
MERCHANT: If you're looking for a place to spend the night, move on! We don't take in beggars!
RABBI ZEV: Beggars! Do you know to whom you are speaking? *(indicates Elijah)* My friend here—
MERCHANT: I am the great Achaz, the wealthiest merchant in all Israel. I need no friends of your ilk.
RABBI ZEV: This is an outrage!
ELIJAH: We do not wish to trouble you, only to speak awhile and gain shelter from the night.
MERCHANT: Well, if that's all you want, you can sleep in the stable with the horses. But don't annoy them with your prattering!

ELIJAH: Toda. May your generosity in this life match your reward in the next.

(Elijah and Rabbi Zev cross a few feet left and lie down.)

RABBI ZEV: *(to Elijah)* I am starving! How can you walk all day without eating?

MERCHANT: And don't think about trying to wangle any food from the cook! *(exits left)*

RABBI ZEV: Miserly ingrate! And did you notice the gate post? It's almost off the hinges! You'd think the wealthiest merchant in all Israel would take better care of his property! What do you think, master? Master? Are you asleep? How can you sleep when I am so hungry?

(Rabbi Zev plops down as LIGHTS FADE DOWN TO HALF.)

SUSANNA: Once again, Rabbi Zev suffered a sleepless night, marred by peculiar dreams. When he awoke, his temper was not improved by his hunger.

(LIGHTS UP LEFT on Rabbi Zev awaking; Elijah is sitting up and staring at the Merchant who stands at down left, pacing as if inspecting the gate post.)

MERCHANT: This is splendid! My gate post has been repaired. It is a miracle! An absolute miracle! *(sees Elijah and Rabbi Zev)* You two beggars! Bedtime is over! Be on your way! Lekh mipo! *(exits left)*

(Elijah and Rabbi Zev stand.)

RABBI ZEV: Great Prophet, I can no longer hold my tongue. It was you who repaired the gate post. How in the world could you do that greedy man a favor and save him an expense he can well afford? And at the same time, cause the death of that poor couple's goat?

ELIJAH: My dear rabbi, you have much to learn, and the virtue of patience should be your first task.

RABBI ZEV: You helped a rich man who treated you badly, and you made life harder for a man and woman who did you no injury at all! What can I learn from that?

ELIJAH: Do you know why we stopped at the house of the old man and old woman? I had seen the Angel of Death hovering on the roof above. Death had come for the wife, but I prayed to God to spare her, and He directed the Angel to take the goat instead.

RABBI ZEV: Thus allowing the old couple to enjoy each other's love and company for many years to come.

ELIJAH: As for the merchant who treated us so badly, I replaced his gate post for this reason. Being of miserly temperament, he would have done the repair himself. Just inside the gate lies a bag of gold coins buried years ago. Once the merchant began digging for the new post—

RABBI ZEV: He would have found the coins and become even more undeservedly rich! Ay! How stupid I have been! All this time in the presence of a great teacher, and I have learned nothing!

ELIJAH: You have learned something very important — the ways of God and His judgments go far beyond the understanding of humankind. When you see a heartless, selfish man who appears to prosper, and a kindly man who appears to be full of sorrow and distress, do not be deceived. It is all part of God's eternal plan, a plan we humans glimpse only as an ant sees the dust from the feet of pilgrims passing along the road.

(LIGHTS DOWN LEFT; SPOTLIGHT UP RIGHT ON Susanna at down left.)

SUSANNA: And that was the last the Rabbi saw of the Prophet, who went around the corner and ascended into heaven on a whirlwind of fiery chariots! *(looks to right)* Oh, here comes my father. I had better get back to work. Come by tomorrow, and I will tell you of the time this fellow Jonah came round looking for a whale harness. Shalom!

(LIGHTS OUT.)

THE END

THE WISDOM OF SOLOMON

The Book of Kings states that Israel's King Solomon was twelve years old when God promised him that he would be granted great wisdom. The story is told that young Solomon was given the choice between wealth and wisdom; when he chose wisdom, God was so pleased that he granted Solomon not only wisdom but also enormous wealth. The son of King David, Solomon ruled Israel from around 970–930 B.C.E., the zenith of Israel's status as a major sovereign kingdom, during which time Solomon built the Temple in Jerusalem. This play contains several quotations from Solomon's Proverbs and the Song of Songs, two Biblical books also believed to have been written by Solomon; check your Scripture and see if you can find them!

STAGE SET: 2 rocking chairs at down right; a small table and stool at down left; a throne at mid center

CAST: 16 actors, minimum 6 boys (•), 9 girls (+)

+ Mrs. Taylor
+ Jayne
• King Solomon (as a child)
• King David
+ Widow +
• Poor Man
+ Poor Man's Wife
+ First Woman

• Mr. Taylor
+ Deborah
• King Solomon (as an adult)
+ Queen Bathsheba
  Neighbor Woman
• Rich Man
  Court Servant
+ Second Woman

PROPS: Book; earthen jar; gold coins; long wooden spoon; hand mirror; a modern toy doll; a plain life-size doll resembling a real baby

COSTUMES: Mrs. Taylor, Mr. Taylor, Jayne, and Deborah wear contemporary clothes. Other characters wear basic Biblical attire befitting their occupation and status — long-sleeved, plain-colored tunics (ankle-length for females, knee-length for males), sandals, a simple cloth or scarf wrapped around the head and shoulders for women, beards for adult men. King David, Queen Bathsheba, and adult King Solomon wear more brightly colored, richly patterned tunics as well as crowns and other royal accessories. Court Servant is like a soldier and wears armor, a helmet, and carries a sword.

GLOSSARY: *chal-la* — a type of braided white bread; *le-hit-ra'ot* — see you later; *met-zu-yan* — excellent; *sha-lom* — hello or good-bye; *Tish-rei* — month of September/October; *far-misht* — confused; *to-da* — thank you; *be-va-ka-sha* — you're welcome

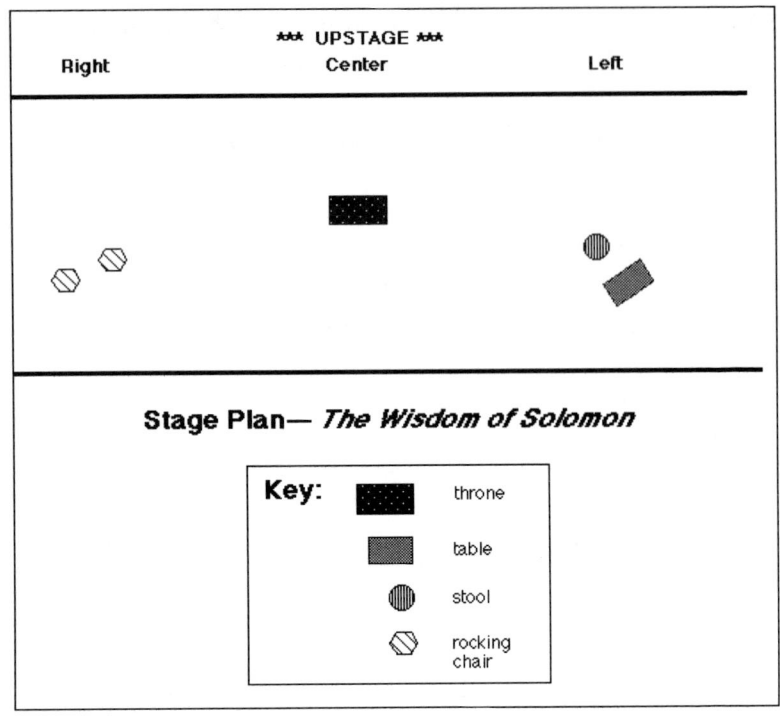

(LIGHTS UP RIGHT ON MRS. TAYLOR and MR. TAYLOR, AN ELDERLY COUPLE, sitting on rocking chairs at down right; Mrs. Taylor is reading a book, Mr. Taylor is dozing.)

MRS. TAYLOR: What a beautiful summer evening! How nice to relax and enjoy the quiet!
MR. TAYLOR: (snores, then snorts but does not fully wake) Hmmm?
MRS. TAYLOR: (leans close to Mr. Taylor) "I sleep, but my heart is awake. Listen! My beloved is knocking."

(FROM OFFSTAGE LEFT COME ARGUING VOICES; two young girls, JAYNE and DEBORAH.)

JAYNE (Offstage): No! You can never have her! Never!
DEBORAH (Offstage): Don't hurt her, please!

(Jayne and Deborah rush onstage from left, Jayne holding a modern toy doll; Mr. Taylor wakes.)

JAYNE: Oh, hi there, Mr. and Mrs. Taylor.
MRS. TAYLOR: Girls, what is the matter?
DEBORAH: I'm sorry! Are we making too much noise?
MRS. TAYLOR: Enough to wake the dead — and Mr. Taylor.
DEBORAH: I lent Jayne my doll, and she won't give it back.
JAYNE: Your doll? Her doll got stolen by the Schulz' rottweiler and eaten all to bits. *(shakes doll)* Now she wants mine!
DEBORAH: Please, be careful!
MRS. TAYLOR: All right, all right, calm down, you're making me farmisht. Mr. Taylor, I think this is a case for King Solomon.
JAYNE: Who's King Solomon?
MRS. TAYLOR: This child doesn't know King Solomon? The horror!
DEBORAH: Wasn't he a person in the Bible? A king of the Israelites in ancient times?
MR. TAYLOR: Oh, he was in the Bible all right, and he was a great king of Israel and more! He was the wisest man who ever lived, for starters. Did you know that Solomon invented chess? He did. And he had magnificent gardens all over the country and flew upon a carpet of gold and silk, sixty miles long and sixty miles wide. The moon remained full during his reign, every night. Why, he spoke the languages of all the animals, and with the power of a magic ring given by the archangel Michael, he enslaved Ashmedai, the king of demons, to help build the Temple on the summit of Mount Moriah.
JAYNE: Huh?
MRS. TAYLOR: Mr. Taylor tends to exaggerate. But he is right about one thing — Solomon was a very wise king, and he began to show his wisdom early in his youth.

The Wisdom of Solomon 113

(LIGHTS FADE OUT RIGHT AND FADE UP LEFT ON A WIDOW entering from left, carrying an earthen jar and crossing to down left, where she stands and examines the jar.)

MRS. TAYLOR: A widow whose husband had recently died was called away from her home to take care of her parents, who were ill. As she would be away for a long time, she decided to put all her gold into a large jar for safekeeping. She filled the jar with honey, which concealed the coins, and then went to her neighbor.

(NEIGHBOR WOMAN enters from left; Widow calls her.)

WIDOW: Kind neighbor, I must go to my parents. Would you please keep this jar of honey for me until I return?
NEIGHBOR WOMAN: Of course I will. Do not worry about a thing. Your honey will be safe at my house.

(Widow gives jar to Neighbor Woman, who places it on table.)

WIDOW: Toda!
NEIGHBOR WOMAN: Lehitra'ot!

(Widow exits left; Neighbor Woman sits on stool.)

MRS. TAYLOR: Time passed by, and one day the neighbor woman was invited to a wedding. She wanted to bake something special — some nice challa, perhaps — but she had run out of honey. Then she remembered the jar the Widow had left.

(Neighbor Woman has been looking around; she spies the jar and picks up a long wooden spoon from the table.)

NEIGHBOR WOMAN: Hmmm, I wonder if I might borrow a bit of honey from the Widow's jar? It's been sitting here such a long time, I wonder if it is even fresh? *(tastes a spoonful of honey)* Mmmm, metzuyan! Very fresh, indeed! *(digs another spoonful and tastes, then shouts)* Owww! My tooth is broken! *(pulls a coin from spoon)* Just a minute! What have we here? A gold coin!

(Neighbor Woman spoons out other coins, then hides them in her tunic.)

MRS. TAYLOR: As soon as she discovered all the widow's gold, the neighbor woman took them for herself and filled up the jar with new honey, so it would look the same as before. A few days later, the widow returned.

(Widow enters from left.)

WIDOW: Thank you so much for keeping my jar of honey.
NEIGHBOR WOMAN: My pleasure! I mean, no problem, bevakasha. Shalom.
WIDOW: Shalom.

(Neighbor Woman hands jar to Widow, then exits left; Widow shakes jar gently, then looks inside and sits down on stool, crestfallen.)

WIDOW: My gold coins! They have been stolen! But how can anyone help me? I have no witnesses. I have no proof. I am ruined! *(sobs)* There is only one thing to do. I will go to the court of King David and Queen Bathsheba and ask them for judgment against my neighbor!

(LIGHTS UP CENTER ON THRONE AT MID CENTER where KING DAVID sits, QUEEN BATHSHEBA standing behind him; Widow crosses to mid center with jar, bows before throne and addresses King and Queen.)

The Wisdom of Solomon   115

WIDOW: My King and Queen, I am a poor widow. I put all my money in this jar of honey for safekeeping and gave it to my neighbor to protect. She discovered the coins and removed them.

(Neighbor Woman enters from left, crosses to mid center.)

NEIGHBOR WOMAN: That is a lie! And this liar has no proof! I demand she be punished for tarnishing my good name!

KING DAVID: Silence! I am inclined to believe this poor widow. But as she can present no proof and no witnesses, how can I rule in her favor?

QUEEN BATHSHEBA: Perhaps there is a way to learn the truth. Let us call our son, Solomon, and ask him to hear this case.

KING DAVID: Solomon? Why, he is a mere boy!

QUEEN BATHSHEBA: Yes, but he is your son, the son of the greatest warrior king Israel has ever seen.

KING DAVID: True. And your son, as well, my wise and beautiful queen. Very well, call Solomon to the court!

(YOUNG SOLOMON enters from left.)

QUEEN BATHSHEBA: There he is! Solomon, come hear the dispute between these two women.

(Young Solomon crosses to throne, bows, and stands at throne, looking over the two women)

NEIGHBOR WOMAN: You expect this child to render judgment in a case this complicated?

YOUNG SOLOMON: The case rests in the hands of God. I place my trust in Him.

KING DAVID: Very well, Solomon. Proceed.

(Young Solomon points to the jar the Widow holds.)

YOUNG SOLOMON: This is the jar you say contained your gold coins?
WIDOW: Yes, my prince. *(hands jar to Young Solomon)*
YOUNG SOLOMON: And you, neighbor — you say this jar contained nothing but honey?
NEIGHBOR WOMAN: That's all I saw! I borrowed about half the honey in the jar for my wedding challa, then replaced it in full.
YOUNG SOLOMON: Very interesting. . .

(Young Solomon holds the jar up and studies it a moment, then allows it to drop on the ground, where it smashes to pieces.)

QUEEN BATHSHEBA: Solomon! What have you done?
YOUNG SOLOMON: If the widow will look at the pieces. . .

(Widow picks up a piece and examines it.)

WIDOW: A gold coin! Stuck to the bottom of the jar! *(picks up another piece)* And here is another!
YOUNG SOLOMON: Whoever took the coins did not find them all. Indeed, you will see imprints of other missing coins etched on the inside of the jar.
NEIGHBOR WOMAN: No one saw me do anything! There are no witnesses!

(Young Solomon holds up two pieces of jar.)

YOUNG SOLOMON: Here are your witnesses! They have no tongue but speak as strongly as a thousand voices! For the Lord gives wisdom, from His mouth come knowledge and understanding.
KING DAVID: He stores up sound wisdom for the upright and is a shield to those who walk blamelessly.

QUEEN BATHSHEBA: Guarding the paths of justice and preserving the way of His faithful ones.

(LIGHTS OUT CENTER AND LEFT, LIGHTS UP RIGHT.)

DEBORAH: Gee, Mrs. Taylor, Solomon *was* pretty wise. I'm glad the widow got her money back.

JAYNE: He made a lucky guess! He tricked the neighbor into admitting she'd taken honey from the jar, which showed she'd had access to the coins. I wouldn't have fallen for that gag!

MR. TAYLOR: Solomon was more than just a clever detective. When he grew up and became King of Israel, his wisdom was very highly sought. There was the time a rich man and a poor man came before his throne.

(LIGHTS OUT RIGHT AND LIGHTS UP CENTER ON KING SOLOMON sitting on his throne; before him stand A RICH MAN and A POOR MAN.)

RICH MAN: Your majesty, I hate to bother you with such a trivial matter, but this beggar is under the false impression I owe him money.

KING SOLOMON: It is the glory of God to conceal things, but the glory of kings to search things out. State your case.

POOR MAN: My king, I only ask to be given what I was promised. On the fourth day of Tishrei, this rich man came to me and offered me one hundred silver shekels if I would go to the top of a nearby mountain.

RICH MAN: And to remain sitting on that mountain from sundown to sunup the next day, without a cloak or fire or food or any item of comfort!

KING SOLOMON: This seems a peculiar sport.

RICH MAN: It is simply my way of giving alms to the poor. They must earn their charity!

KING SOLOMON: Have you not heard it said, "Whoever is kind to the poor lends to the Lord and will be repaid in full?"

POOR MAN: But, my king, I am a poor man. I need the money for my family, and so I consented to do as this rich man asked. I climbed the steep mountain on the coldest night of the year. I sat down on a rock, and I became very hungry. Around midnight it began to rain. I thought I was going to die.

RICH MAN: And then—

(POOR MAN'S WIFE enters from left and approaches the throne, bowing.)

POOR MAN: My wife!

POOR MAN'S WIFE: In the valley far below, I lit a small fire in our hearth with the last scraps of kindling I could find.

POOR MAN: And high atop the mountain, I saw that tiny light shining from the window of our house. That small speck of light allowed me to imagine my wife and children huddled by the fire, hoping and praying—

POOR MAN'S WIFE: That he would be able to survive the bitter cold and lashing rain.

RICH MAN: There, you see! He *was* comforted! He did *not* stay the whole night without comfort, so he does *not* get the hundred shekels!

POOR MAN'S WIFE: But he felt no warming flame upon his cheek, tasted no morsel of food—

RICH MAN: Nevertheless, he was comforted by the sight of the light in his home! Your majesty, do you not agree?

(King Solomon frowns in silence for a moment.)

KING SOLOMON: Many seek the favor of an earthly ruler, but it is from the Lord in heaven that one gets justice. It is said that "A glad heart makes a cheerful countenance" and also that "A cheerful heart has a continual feast."

The Wisdom of Solomon

When one's heart is cheerful because of belief in the Lord, it is certainly comforted, is it not? The rich man denied the poor man physical comforts, and the law allows this. But it would be wrong to forbid comfort from thoughts, especially thoughts of family or of the Lord. The poor man's comfort came not from this world but from heaven. Therefore, I find for the poor man.

RICH MAN: Impossible!

(Poor Man and Poor Man's Wife fall to their knees with joy.)

POOR MAN: Thank you, my king!
POOR MAN'S WIFE: Bless you, wise Solomon!
KING SOLOMON: And I decree that the rich man will pay this poor man not only the one hundred shekels you promised him, but another hundred for trying to shame him before this court.
RICH MAN: Yes, your majesty. *(bows)*
KING SOLOMON: And perhaps you should consider finding other ways to disperse your charity. Those who oppress the poor insult their Maker; those who are kind to the needy, honor Him.

(LIGHTS OUT CENTER AND LEFT, LIGHTS UP RIGHT.)

MR. TAYLOR: Now, there's some wisdom for you!
JAYNE: But how does that help us? Deborah keeps whining about my stupid doll! *(twirls doll by its arm)*
DEBORAH: Please, be careful! Don't hurt the doll!
MRS. TAYLOR: Mr. Taylor, are you thinking what I'm thinking?
MR. TAYLOR: I am indeed, Mrs. Taylor.
MRS. TAYLOR: We have one more tale of Solomon's wisdom that should give you girls all the help you need.

(LIGHTS OUT RIGHT AND LIGHTS UP CENTER ON KING SOLOMON sitting on his throne, A COURT SERVANT standing to his left; before him stand TWO WOMEN; the FIRST WOMAN holds a baby in her arms, keeping it away from the SECOND WOMAN, who tries to look at it; the First Woman is calm in her manner, while the Second Woman is highly agitated.)

MR. TAYLOR: Once upon a time, two women came to King Solomon and stood before him. The first woman said—
FIRST WOMAN: Your majesty, this woman and I dwell in the same house. There is no one else in the house, only the two of us. I gave birth to a child last week — this baby boy I hold in my arms. On the third day after I gave birth, she also gave birth. The son of this woman died during the night. She arose and took my son from my side while I was asleep, and she put her dead son in my arms.
SECOND WOMAN: That is a lie!
FIRST WOMAN: When I woke in the morning, I saw the dead child and was greatly saddened. But when I observed him closely, I realized he was not the son to whom I had given birth.
SECOND WOMAN: It is not so! My son is the live one and your son is the dead one!
FIRST WOMAN: Whereupon I took my son back from her.
SECOND WOMAN: You stole him from my side while I was sleeping!
FIRST WOMAN: Will you listen to these pathetic lies? I am sorry her weak, sickly son is dead, but she cannot have my healthy baby to take its place.
KING SOLOMON: Order, please!

(Court Servant separates Two Women, making them stand 3-4 feet apart.)

KING SOLOMON: This is indeed a complicated problem. Fortunately, I have a very simple solution. Bring me a sword!

(Court Servant gives sword to King Solomon.)

KING SOLOMON: Bring me the infant!

(Court Servant takes baby from First Woman and holds it at arms length in front of King Solomon.)

KING SOLOMON: Each woman claims the child belongs to her. With this sword, I shall cut the child in two parts, so that each woman may have one half of the child.

(King Solomon raises sword in air; Second Woman rushes forward and kneels before Solomon.)

SECOND WOMAN: No! Please, my Lord, give her the child! Do not kill him!
FIRST WOMAN: *(shrugs)* Half a baby is better than none. Go ahead and cut!

(King Solomon holds sword in air, looks at each Woman, then slowly lowers the sword and points to Second Woman.)

KING SOLOMON: *(to Court Servant)* Give the child to this woman, and do not harm it, for she is his rightful mother!
SECOND WOMAN: *(receives baby from Court Servant)* Thank you, wise king! *(bows)*

(Court Servant hustles First Woman offstage left.)

KING SOLOMON: The eyes of the Lord are in every place, keeping watch on the evil and the good. Happy are those who find wisdom and those who get understanding, for their income is better than silver and their revenue better than gold.

(LIGHTS OUT CENTER AND LEFT, LIGHTS UP RIGHT.)

MR. TAYLOR: Some say that King Solomon knew exactly who the real mother was as soon as he saw the two women and how they each treated the child.
MRS. TAYLOR: Solomon could see the truth in a person's face. This was the nature of the special wisdom given to him by God.
MR. TAYLOR: So what's all this hubbub about a doll?
MRS. TAYLOR: Each of these girls claims the doll belongs to her.
MR. TAYLOR: *(rises)* I guess I'd better get my garden shears.
MRS. TAYLOR: The axe would be better. Or maybe the chainsaw.
MR. TAYLOR: You're right. Doll skin can be hard to slice.
DEBORAH: No! She can have the doll! Just don't hurt it!
JAYNE: *(looks closely at the doll)* You know, I think this may really be Deborah's doll.
MRS. TAYLOR: Are you sure, Jayne?
JAYNE: Yes. It probably was my doll that the dog ate. I'll have my dad ask Mr. Schulz if he'll get me a new one.
MR. TAYLOR: Or maybe feed his rottweiler more often!
JAYNE: *(gives doll to Deborah)* Here, Deborah.
DEBORAH: *(accepts doll and hugs it)* Thank you, Jayne. Come on, let's have a tea party! You can be guest of honor!
JAYNE: Okay!

(Jayne and Deborah scamper offstage right.)

MR. TAYLOR: Too bad. I was looking forward to some blazing scissors action! Snip-snip!

MRS. TAYLOR: Mr. Taylor!

MR. TAYLOR: Just kidding, Mrs. Taylor!

MRS. TAYLOR: I wonder if they learned anything from all that tale telling?

MR. TAYLOR: Maybe that you don't wave a doll in front of a hungry rottweiler!

MRS. TAYLOR: *(holds up book)* As the wise King Solomon said, "Arise, my love, my fair one, and come away. Set me as a seal upon your heart."

MR. TAYLOR: *(helps Mrs. Taylor up from chair)* That Solomon sure had a way with words.

(Mr. and Mrs. Taylor exit right, hand in hand; LIGHTS OUT.)

THE END

CHANUKAH: COME LIGHT THE MENORAH!

The religious holiday Chanukah celebrates a thrilling episode in the history of ancient Israel. Beginning in 175 B.C.E, the reign of Seleucid emperor Antiochus IV of Syria brought religious persecution and political terror to the Holy Land. A Jewish resistance group called the Maccabees rose up in opposition, and civil war raged for three years until the Maccabees defeated the last of the Seleucid armies in 164 B.C.E. Originally known as the Days of Dedication, Chanukah was intended to commemorate the Maccabees' restoration of the Temple in Jerusalem. Around 75 B.C.E. the custom of lighting candles became popular, possibly in conjunction with the water libation ceremony of Simchat Bet HaShoavah that occurs during the religious holiday of Sukkot.

STAGE SET: A table and 3 chairs at down right

CAST: 17 actors, minimum 7 boys (•), 3 girls (+)

- Samuel, about age 9
- Samuel's Father
- Judah Maccabee
- Simon
- Jonathan
- Messenger
- 2 Maccabee Soldiers

+ Tirzah, about age 9
+ Samuel's Mother
- Antiochus
+ Melina
- Lysias
- 4 Seleucid Soldiers

EFFECTS: Sound — collage of soldiers talking in low tones, swords clattering, a horse neighing

MUSIC: "Ma-oz Tzur," "Y'Mei Hachanukah"

PROPS: Menorah; 2 dreidels; silver platter; small parchment scroll; dagger; 6 swords; 2 spears; 2 bows; incense stick; incense holder; jar of oil

COSTUMES: Samuel, Samuel's Mother, and Samuel's Father wear contemporary clothes, with Samuel wearing a baseball cap, starter jacket, baggy pants, outlandish sneakers, and a T-shirt with a Nike or other highly visible corporate athletic logo. Maccabees and Tirzah wear basic male Biblical attire — long-sleeved, plain-colored knee-length tunics, sandals; Tirzah as servant wears a scarf over her head. Antiochus and Melina wear brightly colored, richly patterned tunics as well as crowns and other royal accessories. Lysias, Messenger, and Seleucid Soldiers wear armor, helmets and leather leggings.

GLOSSARY: *sev-i-von* — Hebrew for "dreidel"; *sha-lom* — hello or good-bye

(LIGHTS UP RIGHT ON SAMUEL, SAMUEL'S MOTHER and SAMUEL'S FATHER sitting at the dinner table down right. A Chanukah menorah is on the table with the first candle in place and lit.)

SAMUEL'S MOTHER: The first night of Chanukah! I always get a thrill when we light the menorah! Let's just admire it a while before we put it in the window!

SAMUEL'S FATHER: You did a good job lighting the candle, Samuel.

SAMUEL: *(shrugs)* It's no big deal lighting a candle. Why do we celebrate these old holidays, anyway? I mean, all this stuff that happened in ancient times — who cares?

SAMUEL'S MOTHER: Why, Samuel, I'm surprised! Holidays like Chanukah are important. They bring the family together.

SAMUEL'S FATHER: They also remind us of the brave men and women who fought and died over the centuries for the right to worship as they pleased. There are still many people in many parts of the world today who do not enjoy that right.

SAMUEL: *(idly spins a dreidel)* I guess.

SAMUEL'S FATHER: Would you like to play dreidel?

SAMUEL: Nah! Whoever invented that dumb game? *(sighs)* I wish Aunt Harriet would get here with some more Chanukah gelt. Sure helps pad my allowance!

(Samuel's Mother and Father look at each other in disappointment, frown, and shake their heads.)

SAMUEL'S MOTHER: I'll clean up in the kitchen.

SAMUEL'S FATHER: I'll give you a hand. Samuel, please put the menorah in the window when you're done playing with the dreidel.

SAMUEL: Sure, dad.

(Samuel's Mother and Father exit right.)

SAMUEL: Say, mom, those latkes were delicious! There any more? *(rubs stomach, yawns)* Whoa, I'm sleepy! *(spins dreidel and stares at it)* This dreidel is making me dizzy. . . I'm spinning, spinning, spinning. . .

(Samuel rocks and swoons, then lays his head on the table as LIGHTS FLICKER AND GO OUT. SOUND OFFSTAGE: VOICES OF SOLDIERS TALKING IN LOW TONES, SWORDS CLATTERING, A HORSE NEIGHING. LIGHTS FADE UP TO THREE-QUARTER AT CENTER ON Samuel sitting on ground at down center, head between his knees. He wakes groggily and slowly takes in his surroundings. A YOUNG GIRL, TIRZAH, enters from left, creeping stealthily toward Samuel.)

SAMUEL: What am I doing in the park? Gosh, it's warm out! What happened to all the snow? I don't remember that palm tree being there. *(rubs eyes)* Mom? Dad?

(Tirzah shouts and leaps at him, crouching a few feet to his left in an attack position with object clutched in her right hand.)

TIRZAH: Yaaaaa!
SAMUEL: *(recoils and rolls over)* Yaaaaa!
TIRZAH: Death to all invaders!

(She lunges at him but misses as he rolls away)

SAMUEL: Whoa, hey, cut it out! The karate class is Tuesday night at the Y!

(Tirzah stands, regard him closely.)

TIRZAH: You do not look like a Seleucid.

SAMUEL: I don't know what that is, but if it's a bad thing, I never was and don't want to be one ever.
TIRZAH: What is your name?
SAMUEL: Samuel.
TIRZAH: Samuel! Then you are one of us! Come, quickly!
SAMUEL: Hold on! Where are we?
TIRZAH: Outside the walls of Beth-Zur, the Selucid fortress commanded by the evil Viceroy Lysias.
SAMUEL: Oooookay, that's not quite the answer I was looking for, but it'll do for now. What did you say your name was?
TIRZAH: I am Tirzah, daughter of Hannah and Zimri. My father is fighting in the army of Judah Maccabee, which I humbly serve as a messenger and weapon bearer. *(strikes fighting pose)* But I will soon be a warrior!
SAMUEL: *(backs away)* All right, all right, I believe you, you're a warrior! Say, what's that you're trying to brain me with?

(Tirzah opens her hand and shows a dreidel.)

SAMUEL: *(laughs)* A dreidel! I didn't know they made these toys in ancient times—
TIRZAH: *(brandishes dreidel)* The sevivon is a weapon, not a toy! During the early days of the revolt, our warriors would gather in small groups to plan battles. If the emperor's soldiers caught them, the men would spin the sevivon and say they were only playing a game. Hush! Enemy patrols are about, we must return to camp.
SAMUEL: Lead on. By the way, who exactly are *we*?
TIRZAH: We? We are the people of Israel. *(looks at him critically)* What strange attire you possess!
SAMUEL: Uhhh, I was captured by the whatchama-cids. They make all their prisoners dress this way.
TIRZAH: I am not surprised. Not only are the Seleucids trying to destroy our religion, they seek to wipe out every part of our culture, from the food we eat, to the music

we play, to the clothes we wear. *(strikes fighting pose)* We will never submit! We will fight them to the death!

SAMUEL: Isn't there a middle ground between submission and total death?

TIRZAH: Not according to Antiochus, the Seleucid emperor. Just a few days before the last Sabbath, I was in his very court, disguised as a servant to his sister, Princess Melina. I overheard much.

(LIGHTS UP FULL LEFT ON ANTIOCHUS and MELINA standing at down left.)

ANTIOCHUS: I order every Jew in the city of Jerusalem routed out and killed! They want to worship one God? Let them worship *me*, Antiochus of Syria!

MELINA: My brother, restrain your passion! You have already looted their Temple and ransacked their homes and synagogues. You have forbidden them to practice their customs or to keep their Sabbath.

ANTIOCHUS: Under pain of death!

MELINA: But these are your subjects in the kingdom you inherited from your father. How will you keep their loyalty if you oppress them?

ANTIOCHUS: *(chuckles)* My dear sister, you understand so little about the nature of power and how to use it. These Jews, these Maccabees, have sworn to die for their faith? I will give them their chance! Even as we speak, my General Gorgias has them trapped on the plains at Emmaus, ready for the final slaughter!

(Tirzah, carrying a silver platter with a small parchment scroll and wearing a servant's scarf over her head that conceals her face, crosses to down left and bows to Antiochus and Melina.)

MELINA: Ah, one of my handmaidens. Come, girl. You bring a message?

(Tirzah presents platter to Melina, who takes the scroll and reads it.)

MELINA: This says a messenger sent by Gorgias is outside.
ANTIOCHUS: Bid him enter!

(Tirzah bows and backs away to the right)

ANTIOCHUS: Now, sister, you shall see how a great leader claims his destiny. Like Alexander of Macedonia, I will make the earth tremble before me. I will be called Antiochus the Great! No, Antiochus the Magnificent!

(MESSENGER enters from right and presents himself to Antiochus, as Tirzah stands at the edge of the light close to mid center, watching.)

ANTIOCHUS: What news have you from General Gorgias? When am I to accept the surrender of the Maccabees?
MESSENGER: Gorgias is dead and so are ten thousand of his troops!
ANTIOCHUS: What!?!
MESSENGER: The Maccabees have defeated both our armies at Emmaus and are even now marching toward Jerusalem.
ANTIOCHUS: Impossible!

(Antiochus draw a dagger from his tunic and stabs Messenger in the heart; Messenger groans and stumbles offstage left.)

ANTIOCHUS: Gather the rest of my generals! Have them prepare a new army! This war will not end until every Jew in the land of Israel is annihilated!

(LIGHTS FADE OUT LEFT as Antiochus and Melina exit left; LIGHTS UP FULL CENTER ON Samuel and Tirzah at down center.)

SAMUEL: Wow, that Antiochus sure is a mental case! He needs a serious stress management course.

TIRZAH: He is a tyrant but also a coward. He has sent Lysias with a large army to the south, where they await at Beth-Zur.

SAMUEL: I'd like to stay and help, but I have a math test tomorrow and—

(LIGHTS UP LEFT ON JUDAH MACCABEE entering from left, followed by SIMON and JONATHAN; they stand at down left, facing each other in a circle.)

TIRZAH: It is our leader, Judah Maccabee, and his brothers Simon and Jonathan! They are holding a council of war!

JUDAH MACCABEE: My brothers, when our father, Mattathias, began this campaign three years ago, he said: "Let us swear by the Almighty God never to betray our faith." We have kept that vow, and our time of deliverance is now at hand.

SIMON: Once again, we are few in number and face a large army.

JONATHAN: Our men are exhausted and have few weapons.

JUDAH MACCABEE: Do not be afraid. Remember how our ancestors were saved at the Red Sea when Pharaoh pursued them? Remember how David slew Goliath? And how the blasts of the shofar brought down the mighty walls of Jericho? Carry into battle our father's last words — "Serve God with all your heart and soul and bring redemption to Israel!"

(MUSIC: "Ma-oz Tzur" sung by Judah, Simon, and Jonathan and joined by Samuel and Tirzah.)

JUDAH, SIMON, & JONATHAN: *(sing)*
Ma-oz tzur y'shuati l'khanaeh l'shabeiah
Tikon beit t'filati v'sham todah n'zabeiah
L'eit takhin matbeiah mitzar ham'nabeiah
Az egmor b'shir mizmor hanukat hamizbeiah
Az egmor b'shir mizmor hanukat hamizbeiah

SAMUEL & TIRZAH: *(sing)*
O God, my saving stronghold, to praise you is a delight;
Restore my house of prayer where I will offer you thanks.

SAMUEL, TIRZAH, JUDAH, SIMON, & JONATHAN: *(sing)*
When you will prepare havoc for the foe who maligns us,
I will gratify myself with a song at the altar.
I will gratify myself with a song at the altar.

(TWO MACCABEE SOLDIERS enter from left and form a battle line with Simon and Jonthan, Judah in the front. SOUND OFFSTAGE RIGHT: VOICES OF SOLDIERS TALKING IN LOW TONES, SWORDS CLATTERING, A HORSE NEIGHING.)

SIMON: The enemy nears!

(LYSIAS and FOUR SELEUCID SOLDIERS enter from right in tight battle formation)

SAMUEL: Gosh, those are real swords!
TIRZAH: Come with me and help prepare arrows for the archers!

(Tirzah pulls Samuel upstage out of the main battle area.)

LYSIAS: In the name of Antiochus and the Gods of Greece and Syria, attack!

(The Maccabees and Seleucids clash at center stage; Maccabees prevail and Four Seleucid Soldiers die and/or run offstage left; Lysias kneels to Judah at down center and offers his sword in surrender.)

LYSIAS: I, Lysias, viceroy of the Seleucid kingdom, offer my sword in surrender. You are a skilled general, Judah Maccabee.

JUDAH MACCABEE: *(takes sword)* The God of Israel has guided my hand and won this victory today. Now, we must restore the Temple! On to Jerusalem!

(Judah Maccabee exits left, followed by Simon and Jonathan and the Two Maccabee Soldiers prodding Lysias before them.)

TIRZAH: How exciting! I have never been to Jerusalem.

SAMUEL: I have. It's pretty neat. But the cabdrivers are total maniacs!

(Tirzah stares at him, perplexed.)

SAMUEL: I mean, camel drivers. Listen, the Maccabees aren't going to like what they find when they see the Temple. Everything has been destroyed and defiled.

TIRZAH: Then we must warn them! Hurry!

(Tirzah and Samuel cross to down left but are met by Judah and Simon entering from left; Simon carries a stick of incense in an incense holder.)

SIMON: The Temple is desecrated!
JUDAH: We will rebuild.
SIMON: The altar and sacred vessels are in ruins!
JUDAH: Our work will be all the more rewarding because it is for God.

SIMON: I will collect offerings and light incense. *(lights incense stick)*
JUDAH: Jonathan will bring the menorah to celebrate our restoring the Temple.

(Jonathan enters from left holding a jar of oil.)

JONATHAN: Brothers! This is the only jar of oil in the entire Temple that has not been defiled by the enemy! We cannot light the menorah!
SIMON: This jar contains only enough oil for one day! It will take us at least eight days to make a fresh supply of pure oil!

(Samuel steps forward and addresses Judah.)

SAMUEL: Excuse me, Mr. Maccabee, sir?
JUDAH: And who are you, my boy?
TIRZAH: *(steps forward)* This is my friend, Samuel.
SAMUEL: Son of Stanley and Lorraine. Listen, you *have* to light the menorah with *that* jar of oil. It'll burn for eight days, believe me.
JUDAH: How can you be so sure? Are you a prophet sent by God?
SAMUEL: Let's just say I read it in Torah. *(to Tirzah)* What day is today?
TIRZAH: The twenty-fifth day of Kislev.
SAMUEL: *(to Judah)* You have to light the menorah today, sir. Millions of Jews throughout the world are counting on you.
JUDAH: Very well. This boy has a curious aspect of wisdom about him. Come, let us gather at the altar and light the menorah.

(Judah, Simon, and Jonathan exit left.)

Chanukah: Come Light the Menorah! 135

SAMUEL: *(calls after them)* And lights! String up lots of lights all over the place! Remember, it's a festival of lights!

TIRZAH: I am going to try and find my family. Perhaps I will see you at Temple some night.

(Tirzah takes out the dreidel from her tunic and hands it to Samuel.)

TIRZAH: Take this. Wherever your wanderings lead you, may it remind you of this holy day and all it means to the people of Israel. Shalom.

(He takes dreidel, and they hug.)

SAMUEL: Shalom.

(Tirzah exits left.)

SAMUEL: Speaking of heading home, I haven't seen any telephone booths lately. Wonder if there's a fax machine around here? *(wobbles)* Whew, this incense is starting to make me dizzy! *(sits on ground)* Think I'll just sit down a minute and—

(LIGHTS OUT FOR SEVERAL MOMENTS.)

SAMUEL'S MOTHER: Samuel? Samuel! What's going on down there?

(LIGHTS UP RIGHT ON Samuel at table, waking slowly; Samuel's Mother and Samuel's Father enter from right.)

SAMUEL'S FATHER: Son, I thought you were going to put the menorah in the window. It's almost midnight!

SAMUEL'S MOTHER: Are you feeling okay? *(puts palm to his forehead)* You're running a fever. I'll make soup.
SAMUEL: No, I'm okay. I'm fine. I'm, I'm—
SAMUEL'S FATHER: What is it, Samuel? You look like you had a funny dream.
SAMUEL: I hope not. I mean, I hope some of it was true.

(Samuel takes Tirzah's dreidel from his pocket.)

SAMUEL: Say, dad, do you want to play sevivon? I mean, dreidel?
SAMUEL'S FATHER: Sure. *(picks up dreidel and examines it)* This doesn't look like grandpa's old dreidel. Where did this new dreidel come from?
SAMUEL: Oh, it's been around. Mom, are there any more latkes? I've worked up an appetite.
SAMUEL'S MOTHER: I'll make some. Why don't we sing a Chanukah song while we're waiting?

(MUSIC: "Y'Mei Hachanukah" sung by Samuel, Samuel's Mother, and Samuel's Father, joined by All Characters who enter onstage during the song.)

ALL CHARACTERS: *(sing)*
Y'mei hachanukah chanukat mikdasheinu
B'gil u-v'simchah m'malim et libeinu
Laila vayom s'vivoneinu yisov
Sufganiyot nokhal bam larov hairu
Hadliku neirot chanukah rabim
Al hanisim v'al haniflaot asher chol'lu hamakabim

O Chanukah, O Chanukah, come light the menorah
Let us have a party, we'll all dance the hora
Gather round the table, we'll give you a treat
Shiny tops to play with and latkes to eat
And while we are playing, the candles they burn low

Chanukah: Come Light the Menorah! 137

One for each night, they shed a sweet light
To remind us of days long ago

(LIGHTS OUT.)

THE END

Ma-oz Tzur

(traditional, arranged L.E. McCullough)

138 Plays of Ancient Israel

Ma-oz Tzur, pg. 2

Y'Mei Hachanukah

(traditional, arranged L.E. McCullough)

HAIL, QUEEN ESTHER!

Purim is a Jewish holiday that celebrates Queen Esther's role in preventing a massacre of Persian Jews during the 6th century B.C.E. Purim is named from the Hebrew word *pur*, meaning "lots," which was what the minister Haman threw to select the month he would begin massacring Jews. Much merrymaking is associated with this holiday held on the 14th day of Adar, and celebrants are encouraged to send money to friends and family and distribute gifts of food and money to the poor. In the Middle Ages special plays in Yiddish depicting the events of Purim (*purimshpil*) began to be created by yeshiva students, and eventually, professional theater companies. The *purimshpil* is perhaps the earliest example of Jewish theater in Europe and was first documented in a public performance in Ferrara, Italy, in 1567. Both Jewish and Christian audiences attended these early *purimshpiln*, and by the 1700s, the form was widespread in Jewish communities throughout Europe. Even today, at the dawn of the 21st century, new *purimshpiln* are created and performed by theater troupes around the world in honor of the brave Biblical Queen Esther, whose Hebrew name was Hadassah. With its medieval telling of a Bible story, *Hail, Queen Esther!* bridges the transition to the plays in Volume Two in this series, *Plays of Israel Reborn*.

STAGE SET: Drapes or flats conceal a double-seated throne on platform at mid-center, 2 chairs at mid right, a low banquet table at mid left; just above the chairs is a long drape or flat painted to simulate a wall of a theater

CAST: 16 actors, minimum 6 boys (•), 5 girls (+)
- Salomon Usque
- Duke of Ferrara
- Rabbi Yosef/Mordecai
- King Ahasuerus
- Haman
  3 Servants

- Lazaro Graziano
+ Duchess of Ferrara
+ Tamara Graziano/Esther
+ 3 Princesses
  2 Guards

MUSIC: "Chag Purim," "Ani Purim"

PROPS: 3 oranges; sheet of paper; 8-10 *graggars* (noisemakers, rattles); crown; a pair of dice; parchment scroll; 3 plates of *Hammantashen* ("Haman's pockets" — triangle-shaped poppyseed or fruit cookies)

COSTUMES: Salomon Usque, Lazaro Graziano, Tamara Graziano, Rabbi Yosef, Duke and Duchess of Ferrara, and Servants wear late 16th-century costumes befitting their gender and social status. Characters in the *purimsphil* play wear Biblical attire — long-sleeved, ankle-length, plain-colored tunics, sandals, beards for adult men, veils for Princesses. King Ahasuerus wears a brightly colored, richly patterned tunic as well as a crown and other royal accessories. Haman can wear a three-cornered hat. Guards wear tapered, light-fitting trousers in use among Persian soldiers at the time. Queen Esther appears first in a plain tunic, then as Queen in more royal garb with a beaded tunic or scarf.

GLOSSARY: *buo-na se-ra* — good evening (Italian); *sign-o-ras e sign-o-res* — ladies and gentlemen (It.); *graz-ie* — thanks (It.); *di-ver-tir-si* — enjoy yourself (It.); *buff-ó-ne* — clown (It.); *mag-nif-i-co* — magnificent (It.); *pur-im-shpil* —

Purim play (Yiddish); *shme-ge-gge* — an untalented person (Yid.); *klutz* — a clumsy person (Yid.); *Ham-man-ta-shen* — Purim cookies (Yid.); *tal-lit* — prayer shawl (Hebrew)

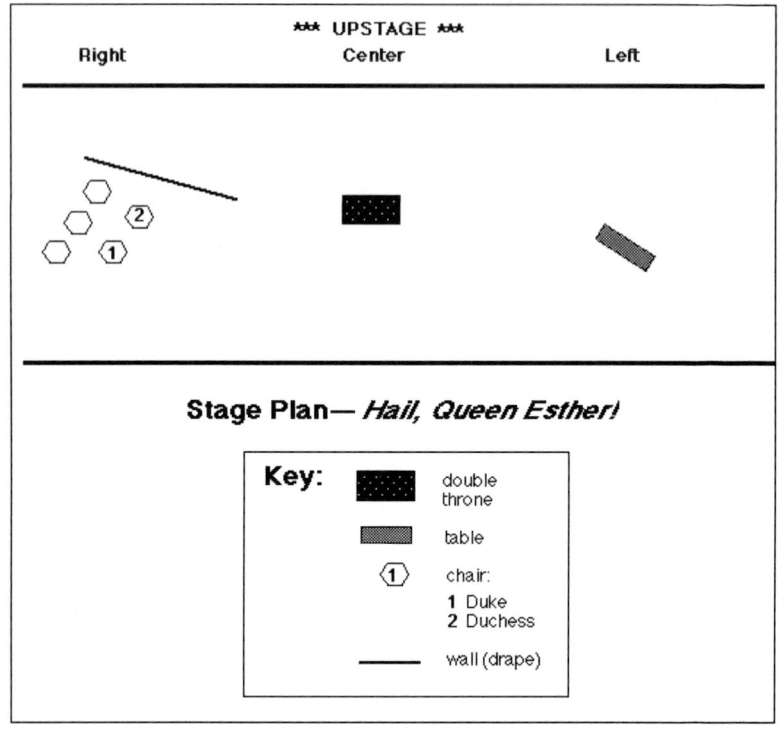

(LIGHTS UP FULL ON SALOMON USQUE standing at down center, facing audience.)

SALOMON USQUE: *(bowing)* Buona sera, signoras e signores. Welcome here this evening to our theater. My name is Salomon Usque, director of one of Europe's most distinguished company of touring actors. We are very pleased to come to your city of Ferrara and perform for your Purim celebration. Here in our Jewish Year 5328, or the year 1567 by the calendar established by the most noble Julius Caesar, we have created a special play—

(LAZARO GRAZIANO has entered from right, awkwardly juggling three oranges and interrupting Salomon; when the oranges fall to the ground, he grins widely and bows with a flourish to the audience and imaginary applause.)

LAZARO GRAZIANO: Thank you, thank you, grazie, grazie! You are too kind!

SALOMON USQUE: Lazaro! What are you doing?

LAZARO GRAZIANO: Practicing for our *purimshpil*, same as you! My juggling act will get the crowd warmed up and ready for excitement!

SALOMON USQUE: Your juggling act will get them heading for the exit. Did we not agree that our play on Queen Esther was to be presented with dignity?

(Lazaro picks up an orange and begins peeling and eating it as he crosses to down center.)

LAZARO GRAZIANO: My poor, poor Salomon — we have travelled together throughout Europe and the Levant, to lands even Marco Polo dared not visit, but you still don't know what satisfies an audience! They want laughs and thrills. They want to be frightened and mystified! Dignity? Who needs it?

(Lazaro slips on an orange peel and spins around crazily before righting himself.)

SALOMON USQUE: Buffóne! Try to be serious for once in your life, Lazaro! The city of Ferrara is ruled by a Duke. This Duke has the reputation of being very severe. Some call him a tyrant. And he is not known to be a friend of the Jews. Fortunately, I have an acquaintance at court, and we have received the Duke's permission to present our play one night only.

LAZARO GRAZIANO: Magnifico! My daughter, Tamara, is ready to play the role of Esther, and I, Lazaro Graziano, will appear as—

SALOMON USQUE: Not so fast. We must still receive permission from the local rabbi, Yosef, or the Jewish community will not be permitted to attend. We will have a play but no audience.

LAZARO GRAZIANO: Trust me, Rabbi Yosef will not be a problem.

SALOMON USQUE: The last time I trusted you, I ended up in the middle of a river with neither a paddle nor a boat!

(RABBI YOSEF enters from left.)

RABBI YOSEF: Is this the lodging of the travelling players?

SALOMON USQUE: Rabbi Yosef! Please enter. We are honored by your visit.
(Rabbi Yosef crosses to down center as Lazaro awkwardly picks up debris from oranges, continuing to comically slip and stumble.)

SALOMON USQUE: We wish to present an entertainment for Purim.

RABBI YOSEF: An entertainment? This is highly irregular! In any case, the Duke would not allow it.

SALOMON USQUE: To the contrary, Rabbi, the Duke has already granted his permission as a boon for his Jewish subjects.

RABBI YOSEF: I do not see how—

SALOMON USQUE: The Christians have their morality plays that tell of saints and miracles. Why should we not celebrate our religious heritage? It will show the Duke we are as clever and talented as any of God's people.

RABBI YOSEF: Plays, entertainments! We have no need of these things! They distract us from what is real in the world!

SALOMON USQUE: And what *is* real in our world, Rabbi? Just last month in Genoa hundreds of Jews were expelled, driven from their homes. In Polotzk thousands of Jews were killed when Ivan the Terrible of Russia conquered the city. And in Cremona, our friendly neighbor to the west, ten thousand Jewish books were burned. Throughout Europe our people are persecuted. More than ever, they need to hear this story of hope and divine protection — the story of Queen Esther and the faithful Mordecai!

RABBI YOSEF: I do not know. I will have to consult Torah on this matter.

(Rabbi Yosef turns away; Lazaro steps forward, nudging and winking at Salomon.)

LAZARO GRAZIANO: Salomon, have you ever noticed what a remarkable resemblance Rabbi Yosef holds to Mordecai?

SALOMON USQUE: Why, yes, now that you mention it, my dear Lazaro, the Rabbi bears a striking likeness to the bold Mordecai.

(Rabbi Yosef half turns, noticing their conversation and becoming more and more puffed up by their flattery.)

LAZARO GRAZIANO: The wise Mordecai.
SALOMON USQUE: The handsome Mordecai.
LAZARO GRAZIANO: The Mordecai whom the people hailed as their protector.
SALOMON USQUE: And who so resembles our own Rabbi Yosef.
LAZARO GRAZIANO: Down to the very tip of his tallit!
SALOMON USQUE: If we were to present this play, Lazaro — not that we would do such a thing without the Rabbi's permission — who would you choose to play Mordecai?

Hail, Queen Esther!

LAZARO GRAZIANO: The wise, bold, handsome Mordecai whom the people—
SALOMON USQUE: The very same!
LAZARO GRAZIANO: Oh, I don't know. I suppose that young lad who works at the stable.

(Rabbi Yosef whirls around.)

RABBI YOSEF: Nonsense! No sapling of a boy can equal my experience! I was born to play the role of Mordecai! The people demand it!
SALOMON USQUE: Then play it you shall, Rabbi! *(thrusts a sheet of paper into Rabbi Yosef's hands)* Here are your lines, we begin rehearsal tonight.

(Lazaro gently pushes Rabbi Yosef offstage left.)

LAZARO GRAZIANO: And send us a dozen of your best yeshiva students. Ones that can move and express themselves with ease and grace. No shmegegges or klutzes!
RABBI YOSEF: Yes, of course, I have several in mind.
LAZARO GRAZIANO: Magnifico! See you later!

(Rabbi Yosef exits left.)

LAZARO GRAZIANO: I told you we would have no problem with the Rabbi!
SALOMON USQUE: That was too simple. Somewhere, somehow, something is going to go wrong. I feel it in the wind!
LAZARO GRAZIANO: *(sniffs the air)* I think that is the odor of tonight's supper.

(TAMARA GRAZIANO rushes in from right, gasping.)

TAMARA: Father, father!

LAZARO GRAZIANO: My daughter, Tamara. How delightful to see you! You bring us news?
TAMARA: The Duke of Ferrara is coming!
LAZARO GRAZIANO: What? Here? Now? With soldiers?
TAMARA: No! No!
SALOMON USQUE: That is a relief. For a moment, I thought she said the Duke was coming straight away!
TAMARA: Not now! To the play! He is coming to see the play!
SALOMON USQUE & LAZARO GRAZIANO: The play!?!

(Lazaro faints and falls in Salomon's arms; LIGHTS OUT AS MUSIC ["Chag Purim"] PLAYS AND IS SUNG OFFSTAGE BY THREE PRINCESSES AND TWO GUARDS while drapes or flats are removed to reveal theater sets at mid center, mid right and mid left.)

THREE PRINCESSES & TWO GUARDS (Offstage): *(sing)*
Chag Purim, Chag Purim, Chag gadol hu la-y'hudim,
Masechot, ra'ashanim, z'mirot rikudim.
Hava narisha, rash, rash, rash!
Hava narisha, rash, rash, rash!
Hava narisha, rash, rash, rash!
Bara-ashanim!

Purim is a holiday when we sing and feast and dance!
Masks and songs, food and drink, join us in our glee!
Come, let us tell of bravery!
Watch as the evil Haman flees!
Hail to Queen Esther and Mordecai,
Standing strong and true!

(LIGHTS UP FULL on a theater set — a double-seated throne on platform at mid center and a low banquet table at mid left; at mid right are two chairs. THREE COURT SERVANTS enter from right and stand at down right as they announce to the audience.)

Hail, Queen Esther! 149

COURT SERVANT #1: Signoras e signores, your attention please!
COURT SERVANT #2: We announce the arrival of the Duke of Ferrara!
COURT SERVANT #3: And his lovely and charming wife, the Duchess of Ferrara!
COURT SERVANT #1: Please stand and give polite, respectful applause!
COURT SERVANT #2: So that your taxes are not raised!
COURT SERVANT #3: Nor your children sent to fight the King of Spain!

(The DUKE OF FERRARA and DUCHESS OF FERRARA enter from right, assisted by the Court Servants; Court Servant #1 ushers them into the two chairs, the Duchess in the upper chair, then the Duke in the lower chair; Court Servant #2 prompts the audience to applaud; Court Servant #3 opens a parasol and holds it over the heads of the Duke and Duchess, who wave to the audience.)

DUKE OF FERRARA: Thank you, thank you! Please be seated!

(Court Servants stand behind Duke and Duchess; Duchess waves parasol away and gestures to Court Servant #3 to close it; Salomon Usque enters from left and stands at down left, looking expectantly toward the Duke.)

DUKE OF FERRARA: *(with a flourish)* Let the play begin!

(Audience applauds as Salomon Usque crosses to down center.)

SALOMON USQUE: Signoras e signores, Duke and Duchess, it is our pleasure tonight to bring you a thrilling tale of romance and intrigue from ancient Persia. Prepare to be carried away—

(Lazaro Graziano enters from left in jester's outfit bearing an armful of graggars, which he tosses out to the audience.)

LAZARO GRAZIANO: Halloo! Hallay! Divertirsi! Divertirsi!
SALOMON USQUE: Lazaro! What are you doing!
LAZARO GRAZIANO: I am giving out graggars! *(to audience)* Every time you hear the name "Haman" spoken during the play, you must shake your graggar and make noise to blot out the sound of his name from the heavens! Like this! Haman!

(Lazaro shakes his graggar; the audience shakes their graggars in response.)

LAZARO GRAZIANO: Magnifico!
SALOMON USQUE: Now that you have instructed us all in the art of graggaring, may we continue with the play?
DUKE OF FERRARA: Ahem! The Duchess would like to know if you have any more, how you say, "graggars"?

(Lazaro crosses to right to give a graggar to the Duchess but Court Servant #1 steps in front of him blocking his way; Lazaro gives the graggar to Court Servant #1, who hands it to Court Servant #2, who hands it to Court Servant #3, who hands it to the Duke, who presents it to the Duchess, who accepts it and smiles.)

DUCHESS OF FERRARA: Grazie!

(Lazaro bows deeply and falls over to great laughter among audience; he picks himself up and exits right as Salomon begins crossing to stand at down right, speaking as he walks.)

SALOMON USQUE: Many centuries ago, in the faraway land of Persia, there was a king by the name of Ahasuerus.

(KING AHASUERUS enters from behind wall at up right, followed by TWO GUARDS, and crosses to sit on throne with a Guard on either side; a crown sits on the vacant part of the throne next to King Ahasuerus.)

SALOMON USQUE: After a dispute with his wife, Queen Vashti, he banished her from the kingdom. And then, naturally, he sought a new queen to take her place.
KING AHASUERUS: I need a new queen! Send for all the young women in Persia, and have them brought here. I will interview them and see which is worthy to be queen.

(Guard #1 exits left.)

KING AHASUERUS: *(to Guard #2)* I will need some additional advice on this matter. Send for my chief adviser, Haman.

(Lazaro pops out from curtain at down right and waves a graggar, egging on the audience to do the same. Salomon tries to shush Lazaro and audience but fails as Guard #2 exits up right.)

KING AHASUERUS: And of course, I shall need the services of the court scribe, Mordecai. I wonder where he can be?

(MORDECAI enters from left and stands at down left.)

MORDECAI: *(to audience)* I am Mordecai. I am a Jew, whose family came to Persia many years ago after our Temple in Jerusalem was destroyed by Babylonian invaders. Many Israelites live here in Persia, where the king has been fair and tolerant to all his subjects — until now.

(Guard #1 enters from left leading THREE PRINCESSES, who cross to down center, where they bow and present themselves to King Ahasuerus; Guard #1 stands to left of throne.)

KING AHASUERUS: Ah, yes, here come the princesses of Persia!

(Guard #2 enters from up right, followed by HAMAN, who approaches the throne and bows to King Ahasuerus; Guard #2 stands to right of throne.)

KING AHASUERUS: And now has arrived my adviser, Haman.

(Lazaro pops out from curtain at down right and waves a graggar, egging on the audience to do the same. Salomon throws up his hands in futility.)

HAMAN: I am here, your majesty, to assist in any way. Especially if it confounds your enemies.

KING AHASUERUS: Enemies? *(laughs)* But I am not preparing for war. I am seeking a new queen. Let us review the candidates!

(Three Princesses dance and twirl in place as King Ahasuerus and Haman watch them. MUSIC PLAYS OFFSTAGE: instrumental version of "Chag Purim." ESTHER enters from left and approaches Mordecai at down left.)

MORDECAI: Esther, my beautiful niece!
ESTHER: Mordecai, my wise uncle!
MORDECAI: The king is choosing a new queen. You must present yourself to the court.
ESTHER: But Uncle, to tout my beauty in such a manner would be vain!

MORDECAI: It is for the well-being of your people. You must!

ESTHER: Very well, dear Uncle. I will do according to your will, and to God's.

MORDECAI: Go then, but tell no one you are a Jew. There are those at court who seek to harm our people.

(Music stops; Princesses stop moving and kneel before throne.)

KING AHASUERUS: *(to Haman)* What do you think of these princesses?

HAMAN: Well—

KING AHASUERUS: They are all very beautiful, I suppose. But I fear none are worthy to serve as my queen.

HAMAN: Perhaps—

(Mordecai steps forward, Esther behind him.)

MORDECAI: Your majesty! I have a candidate!

KING AHASUERUS: Ah, it is my court scribe, Mordecai! Welcome! Who is this lady you bring forth?

(Esther steps forward, bowing; King Ahasuerus stands in surprise and rapture.)

ESTHER: My name is Esther.

KING AHASUERUS: Esther! That is not a name but a melody. A melody that sings to the deepest shadow of my heart!

HAMAN: Your majesty—

KING AHASUERUS: *(claps hands)* The contest is over! I choose Esther for my queen

HAMAN: But your majesty!

MORDECAI: The king has spoken! Hail, Queen Esther! *(to audience)* Hail, Queen Esther!

(Lazaro pops out from curtain at down right and encourages audience to shout along.)

LAZARO GRAZIANO: Hail, Queen Esther! Hail, Queen Esther!

(Princesses make way for Esther, who crosses to throne and kneels before King Ahasuerus; he puts crown on Esther's head.)

KING AHASUERUS: I crown thee, Esther, Queen of Persia!
PRINCESSES, GUARDS, & MORDECAI: Hail, Queen Esther!

(Esther sits on throne next to King Ahasuerus as Princesses exit up right; Haman crosses to down center and speaks to audience.)

HAMAN: We shall see about this new queen who Mordecai has conveniently discovered! *(exits up right)*

(Mordecai crosses to down left and turns to left as Two Guards sneak away from throne and meet at mid left by banquet table; King Ahasuerus and Esther sit on throne, frozen in place, holding hands.)

SALOMON USQUE: Not long after, Mordecai was in a remote part of the palace and overheard two of the king's guards at mischief.
GUARD #1: Is everything ready?
GUARD #2: We strike tonight! The king will be murdered in his sleep!

(Mordecai crosses to down center as the Two Guards exit left; Mordecai beckons to Esther, who leaves the throne and joins him at down center.)

Hail, Queen Esther! 155

MORDECAI: Dear niece, there is a plot to murder the king!
ESTHER: I will inform him at once!
MORDECAI: Do so, but be careful of who else hears.

(Mordecai crosses to down left as Esther returns to throne, whispers in King Ahasuerus' ear; angered, the King rises.)

KING AHASUERUS: Death to all traitors! Have the plotters arrested and killed at once!

(Haman enters from up right.)

HAMAN: It is fortunate, my king, that this plot was prevented.
KING AHASUERUS: And it is my loyal queen who saved the day. We should all be so alert, chief adviser!
HAMAN: Yes, your majesty.
KING AHASUERUS: Carry on, as you were.

(King Ahasuerus and Esther exit up right; Haman bows as they exit, then crosses to down center and commands Mordecai.)

HAMAN: You, scribe! Come here!

(Mordecai crosses to down center.)

HAMAN: As chief adviser to the king, I order you to bow down before me.
MORDECAI: That I cannot do, chief adviser.
HAMAN: And who are you to disobey me?
MORDECAI: I am Mordecai the Jew. My people do not bow in worship to men. We pray only to Almighty God, the one true God of all humankind.

(Mordecai bows and exits left as Haman seethes with fury.)

HAMAN: I will have revenge upon this Mordecai and his people! I will tell the king that the Jews are plotting to overthrow the kingdom! And the king will give me full power to kill every Jew in Persia! *(laughs maniacally)* Let me see, when should this massacre begin? *(takes a pair of dice from his cloak)* I shall cast lots. *(kneels on ground)* The month of Tishri? *(rolls dice)* No, too close to the harvest. The month of Tebet? *(rolls dice)* Too cold! How about the month of Adar? *(rolls dice)* Yes! Perfect! When spring comes, Jewish blood will flow! *(exits up right)*

SALOMON USQUE: And so this evil minister told the king that there were enemies within Persia seeking to destroy the empire. He succeeded in getting permission from the king to deal with the matter. Without the king's knowledge, he issued a decree that on the thirteenth day of the month of Adar, the Jews of Persia would be killed. When Queen Esther heard the decree, she sent for Mordecai.

(Esther enters from up right, Mordecai enters from left; they meet at mid left by banquet table.)

ESTHER: Uncle, the king has signed a terrible decree!

MORDECAI: I have heard. But the king does not know it is intended to massacre the Jews. You must persuade the king to take back his order.

ESTHER: Though the king loves me very much, I cannot speak to him unbidden on matters of state. If I displease him, I could be put to death!

MORDECAI: It is a risk you must take, my niece — for the sake of our people.

(Mordecai exits left.)

ESTHER: Mordecai is right. I cannot stand and watch as my people are destroyed by lies. I would rather disobey the king and die than let my people perish. I will fast and pray for three days and then request an audience with the king.

(Esther kneels; King Ahasuerus enters from up right, followed by Haman, and sits on throne with Haman standing to his right.)

KING AHASUERUS: The queen wishes to address me on matters of state?
ESTHER: Your majesty, I wish to invite the king and his chief adviser to a banquet I have prepared in your honor.
KING AHASUERUS: I accept the invitation.
HAMAN: As do I, your majesty.

(King Ahasuerus crosses to banquet table and sits next to Esther, who whispers in his ear as Haman steps forward to down center and soliloquys to audience.)

HAMAN: I know the purpose of this banquet! I will be rewarded for my efforts in ridding the kingdom of Jews! After my reward, I shall request the death of Mordecai. Let me see, how shall he die? I think the gallows would suffice! *(laughs maniacally)*

(Haman crosses to banquet table, bows, and remains standing.)

KING AHASUERUS: Chief adviser, if you were king, how would you best show your gratitude to a man who has loyally served his ruler?
HAMAN: Gratitude? Well, I would dress him in the finest of robes and place a crown on his head. I would set him upon the king's finest horse and appoint the highest-ranking prince to lead him throughout the city calling so

all the people could hear: "Here is the man the king sees fit to honor above all others!" *(chuckles)* Oh, yes, that is how I would reward such a great man.

KING AHASUERUS: Those are excellent suggestions, chief adviser. Now, join me in honoring a great man — the court scribe, Mordecai!

(Mordecai enters from left and Haman recoils in shock.)

HAMAN: Mordecai!

KING AHASUERUS: Mordecai was the man who discovered the plot to kill me. He is one of my most loyal servants.

HAMAN: But—

KING AHASUERUS: Chief adviser, prepare to bestow the highest honors of Persia upon Mordecai.

HAMAN: But your majesty, there is a decree—

KING AHASUERUS: A decree?

ESTHER: A decree has been issued in your name to kill all the Jews on the thirteenth day of Adar. And Mordecai is a Jew.

KING AHASUERUS: What?

ESTHER: And I, your queen — I, too, am a Jew. And, therefore, must die with my people.

KING AHASUERUS: *(stands)* This decree must be withdrawn at once! Who is responsible for such an abomination?

ESTHER: *(points to Haman, who has moved toward down center)* This evil man, your majesty. Your chief adviser, Haman!

(Audience shake their graggars, led by Duchess of Ferrara, who stands and vigorously shakes her graggar.)

KING AHASUERUS: Guards! Seize this man and send him to the gallows! He — and not the Jews — is the true enemy of my kingdom!

Hail, Queen Esther! 159

(Two Guards enter from left and grab Haman, dragging him offstage up right; Three Princesses enter from left, each bearing a plate of Hammantashen they place on the table.)

KING AHASUERUS: I appoint Mordecai my new chief adviser. And to my queen, Esther, I give thanks for her wisdom and loyalty.

ESTHER: Thank you, your majesty. Will you try a new delicacy?

(Esther offers the King a Hammantashen; he samples it.)

KING AHASUERUS: This is delicious! What do you call this delightful pastry?

ESTHER: Hammantashen — Haman's pockets.

(Audience shake their graggars, led by Duchess of Ferrara, who stands and vigorously shakes her graggar as Lazaro Graziano joins Salomon Usque at down center.)

SALOMON USQUE: And so our drama ends tonight, with evil yielding to force of right.

LAZARO GRAZIANO: We hope this play much pleasure brought, giving wholesome food for thought.

(Salomon and Lazaro turn to Duke and Duchess.)

SALOMON USQUE: And to our patrons noble and kind,
LAZARO GRAZIANO: We pray in grace their favor find.

(Salomon and Lazaro bow to Duke and Duchess.)

DUKE OF FERRARA: This play was very interesting. Does the Duchess agree?

DUCHESS OF FERRARA: Indeed! Someday I should like to play the role of Queen Esther!

DUKE OF FERRARA: As long as it be on stage and not off.

(Duchess frowns at Duke a moment without reply, then shakes her graggar in his face; Duke laughs and all characters enter and sing. MUSIC: "Ani Purim.")

ALL: *(sing)*
Ani Purim, ani Purim
Saméach umvadéach
Halo rak paam bashana
Avo l'hitaréch

La-la-la-la-la-la!
La-la-la-la-la!
La-la-la-la-la-la!
La-la-la-la!
It would be fun if Purim came once a month or twice a week!
Let's make each day a day of joy, all hail Queen Esther's miracle!

La-la-la-la-la-la!
La-la-la-la-la!
La-la-la-la-la-la!
La-la-la-la!

(LIGHTS OUT.)

THE END

Ani Purim

(traditional, arranged L.E. McCullough)

Hail, Queen Esther!

L.E. McCULLOUGH, PH.D., is an educator, playwright, composer, and ethnomusicologist whose studies in music and folklore have spanned cultures throughout the world. Dr. McCullough is the Administrative Director of the Humanities Theatre Group at Indiana University-Purdue University at Indianapolis. Winner of the 1995 Emerging Playwright Award for his stage play *Blues for Miss Buttercup*, he is the author of *The Complete Irish Tinwhistle Tutor*, *Favorite Irish Session Tunes*, and *St. Patrick Was a Cajun*, three highly acclaimed music instruction books. He has performed on the soundtracks for the PBS specials *The West*, *Lewis and Clark*, and *Not for Ourselves Alone: The Story of Elizabeth Cady Stanton and Susan B. Anthony*. Since 1991 Dr. McCullough has received 45 awards in 31 national literary competitions and had 178 poem and short story publications in 90 North American literary journals. He is a member of The Dramatists Guild, American Conference for Irish Studies, Southeastern Theatre Conference, and National Middle School Association. His books for Smith and Kraus include: *Plays of the Songs of Christmas*; *Stories of the Songs of Christmas*; *Ice Babies in Oz: Original Character Monologues*; *Plays of America from American Folklore, Vol. 1 & 2*; *Plays of the Wild West, Vol. 1 & 2*; *Plays from Fairy Tales*; *Plays from Mythology*; *Plays of People at Work*; *Plays of Exploration and Discovery*; *Anyone Can Produce Plays with Kids*; *Plays of Ancient Israel*; *Plays of Israel Reborn*; *111 One-Minute Monologues for Teens, Vol. 2*; and *"Now I Get It!": 12 Ten-Minute Classroom Drama Skits for Elementary Science, Math, Language & Social Studies, Vol. 1 & 2*.